When a piece of art speaks volumes without uttering a single word, there you have revealed from your inner self a true connection to your higher power.

Your thoughts are conveyed from the soul of who you really are. Your hands have become the tools designed for the purpose of creating your own personal reality.

Let your heart speak… Let your soul listen.
Carry out the will and desires of your inner self.
"Follow your heart" is the motto "LIVED" by this remarkable ART genius.
Her name ….. it is …. **"Vladlena"**.

There is a great EXTREME to the creations she has bestowed upon the art world. Depth and width do not comply to her work. It has no boundaries. She unleashes a message of the eternal.

Each art piece is so intricate and detailed to the extreme. It is versatile and is a mere surprise to the viewer. The mystery is hers to give…with her genuine and deliberate intentions….At times… she reveals a shocking and strangely wonderful appeal to her work.

Vladlena lives in Latvia. She has always loved art and began drawing at a young age. In 2007 she began to create dolls and figurines in paper clay and Living Doll clay, which is done over wire armatures. The captivating shapes and unusual curves to some of her art pieces give them a total uniqueness. Some of her pieces are cast from her own molds. Most of her work is freehand and is created spontaneously. Her interest's in history and studying the backgrounds of the mystical world are mixed with realism which has given her much inspiration. Her highest hopes are to touch others in a profound way with her art.

She has an AMAZING Gallery which displays her brilliant artwork . Each piece is carefully placed with just the right lighting to bring emphasis to each and every detail. Her creations are unique in every way,

Vladlena gives wonderful tribute to the world of ART. Thank you "Vladlena" for sharing the utmost part of yourself with us for all to enjoy. Your work inspires us and takes us to places that unfold new worlds of excitement.

If you wish to visit her Gallery you may contact her through her web site.
http://vladlenadoll.com You will also find many photos of her art pieces.

Written by Vikki Ebbeling, IDA Magazine Writer

Vladlena's One of a Kind Dolls

Vladlena began making author's dolls in 2007. She is a Member of the Art dolls section of the Creative Union of Russia. Also she is a member of the Professional Doll Makers Art Guild and won the highest fantasy award in the most recent Annual Gold Contest.

Vladlena, who has her own doll gallery in Preili, is a member of the International Author Doll Association (IADA) and a member of the Baltic Guild of Doll and Toy Artists. The President of Latvia, Valdis Zatlers, ordered a doll in 2009 that became a gift to King Juan Carlos of Spain.

Vladlena's dolls are very popular. They are displayed in galleries in Moscow and Baku as well as in private collections in many countries of the world: England, Ireland, France, Germany, Russia, Belarus and the United States. Vladlena has participated in many international exhibitions - in Riga, Prague, Moscow, Tallinn, St. Petersburg, Baku, Minsk, Vilnius, Amsterdam and Muenster. She has also won prizes in various competitions.

In 2009 she won the main Prize of the Doll Master magazine. A Prizewinner in the Our Childhood Fairytale and Anti-stress Doll categories at the 1st international Dolls Seasons in Riga exhibition.

In 2013 she won the details category and the audience's choice Prize in the Del Arte competition,

In 2014 she won a prize in the 10th anniversary international Salon of Dolls exhibition in Moscow.

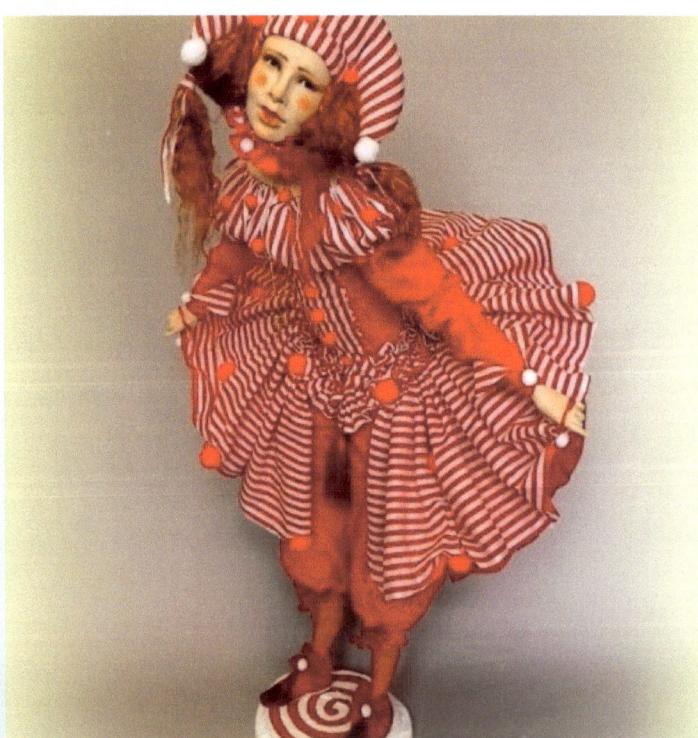

The audience's choice prize at the Panna DOLL'ya exhibition in Minsk, a prize at the Kingitus Christmas exhibition in Tallinn and a Prize for charitable contribution to helping children in Tallinn.

In 2015 she won the audience's choice prize at the 1st international Doll Summer in Preili festival. She also participated in a charity event to support children with cancer in Riga, which was held in Riga's Grand Hotel. Author's dolls by Vladlena were shown at the international Kingitus exhibition in Tallinn. Preili Municipality Council awarded Elena Mikhaylova (Vladlena) the rank of Honorable Citizen of the Preili Municipality on June 19 2015. She received this honor for her contribution to the popularization of Preili region and for socially important and creative work in the development of tourist activity.

In August 2015 and 2016, Vladlena was one of the organizers of the international Doll Summer festival in Preili.

Written by Vikki Ebbeling, IDA Magazine Writer

Dear Readers,

It is with grateful hearts that we thank all of our subscribers for your support. It is our goal to represent the many artists in the art doll industry.

Subscribe by visiting our website.

internationaldollartists@gmail.com

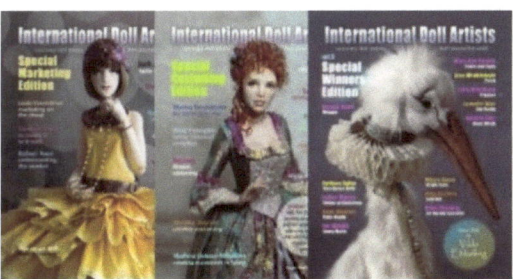

Quarterly Magazine

Publishing Dates:

January, April, July, October

Digital downloads and hard copies available

Copyright © 2017 by Cherie Fretto, Professional Doll Makers Art Guild. All rights reserved. No part of this publication may be reproduced, distributed, or transmitted in any form or by any means, including photocopying, recording, or other electronic or mechanical methods, without the prior written permission of the publisher, except in the case of brief quotations embodied in critical reviews and certain other noncommercial uses permitted by copyright law. For permission requests, write to the publisher, addressed "Attention: Publisher," at the email address below. Publisher is not responsible for unsolicited materials. Product names used are used with permission of the copyright and trademark holders, for editorial use only. No further rights are implied. All subscriptions are by download only, with printed copies on demand. Delivery will be four times a year as stated on our website. An email will be delivered to notify you of accessibility.

IDA Publishing ©

internationaldollartists@gmail.com
www.internationaldollartists.com

Published and printed in the USA.

Who is IDA Magazine?

Cherie Fretto: Publisher/Editor

Cherie is the President and CEO of the Professional Doll Makers Art Guild. She has received many Diamond Award for her OOAK polymer clay dolls, but specializes in BJDs, where she does her own molding and casting for limited resin editions.

www.BJDStudio.com

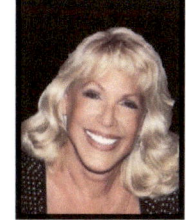

Peggy McChesney: Managing Editor/ Graphic Designer

Peggy is the Treasurer and Membership Chairperson for the Professional Doll Makers Art Guild and a One of a Kind Doll and Teddy Bear Artist specializing in Babies, Children, needle felting and mohair plush.

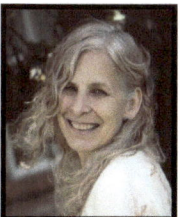

Lisa Wroblewski: Art & Education Editor

Lisa is an artist following her true passion for sculpting, specializing in One of a Kind and limited edition dolls. She also loves sharing her knowledge through teaching other artists on their sculpting journey.

www.cecilandco.com

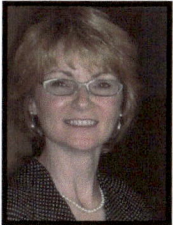

Gayle Wray: Cover Graphic Designer

Gayle is an award-winning artist and graphic designer, author, and master cloth doll artist. She I the recipient of the Light Space & Time solo-artist showcase award and her dolls have been featured at the Ontario Museum of History & Art.

www.gaylewray.com

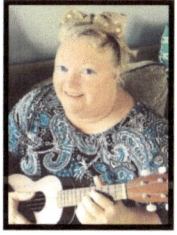

Lynn Jacobs: IDA Contributing Writer

Lynn is a Painter, Sculpturist, Artist, Writer and retired 26 years ABCH Master Haircolorist. She enjoys learning, being inspired and coming up with unique, one-of-a-kind ideas and creations. She creates mermaids and fantasy characters in polymer clay and loves sharing her knowledge and musings with others.

www.facebook.com/LindaLynnJacobs

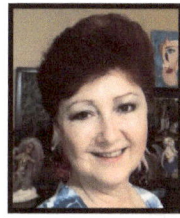

Vikki Ebbeling: IDA Feature Writer

Wife... Mother... Grandmother... and Master Doll Maker and Writer. Her desires are to portray an utmost realism to her art and create a profound connection to people depicting the miracle of "Life" to be the greatest gift of all.

www.uniquedollsnteddys.com

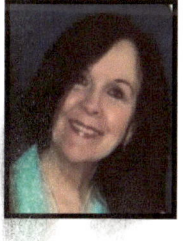

International Doll Artists - September 2018—Volume 4

Articles

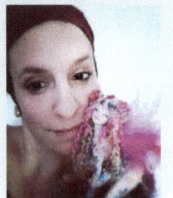
Elisabetta Visentini
Accessories Are A Passion
Pages 18-19

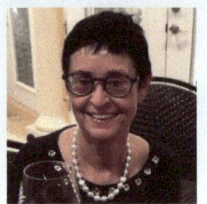
Ankie Daanen
High Heel Shoes
Page 56-58

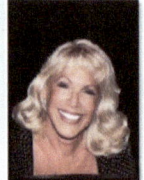
Cherie Fretto
Working With Worbla
Page 28-29

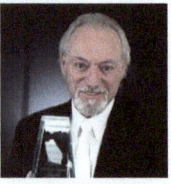
Jack Johnston
Icing On The Cake
Pages 16-17

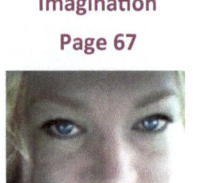
Cherie' Davidson
Using Your Imagination
Page 67

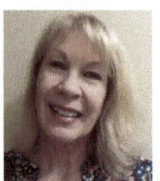
Leann Marshall
Inspiring With Accessories
Page 24-26

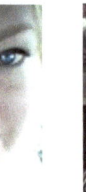
Lisa Wroblewski
Making a Doll Purse
Pages 20-22

Gayle Wray
Tuffet Love
Page 48-51

Dennis Slate
Love Them or Hate Them
Page 35

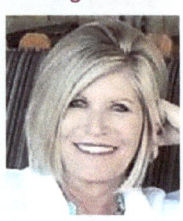
Shauna McCullough
Land Of Make Believe
Page 42-45

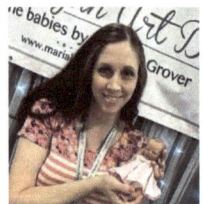
Maria Grover
Casting Accessories
Page 40-41

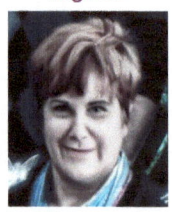
Lesley Duthie
Dancing Shoes
Page 30-34

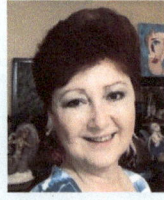
Lynn Jacobs
Opal Mermaid Tail
&
Directing The Viewer
Page 62-66

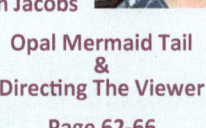

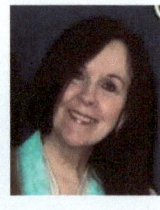
Vikki Ebbeling
"Meet Vladlena"
&
Working with Colors
Page 3-4, 53

What's Inside

Vladlena Beyond Amazing

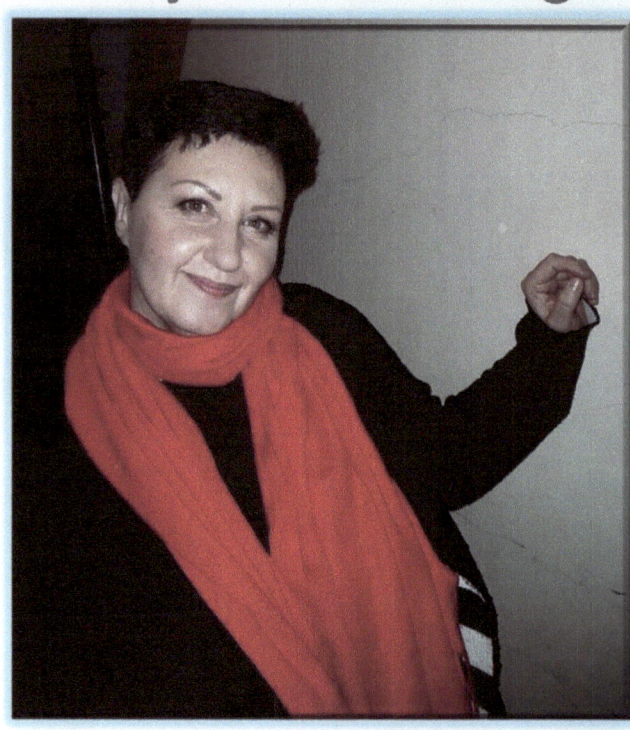

Professional Doll Makers Art Guild
Top Fantasy Artist 2017

Pages 3-12

Vladlena is a receiver of the official "*Master Artist*" logo through the Professional Doll Makers Art Guild.

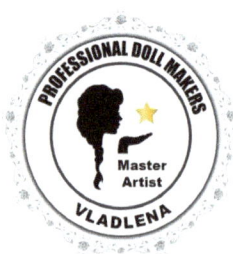

"If you ask me what I came to do in this world, I, an artist, will answer you: I am here to live out loud."
— Émile Zola

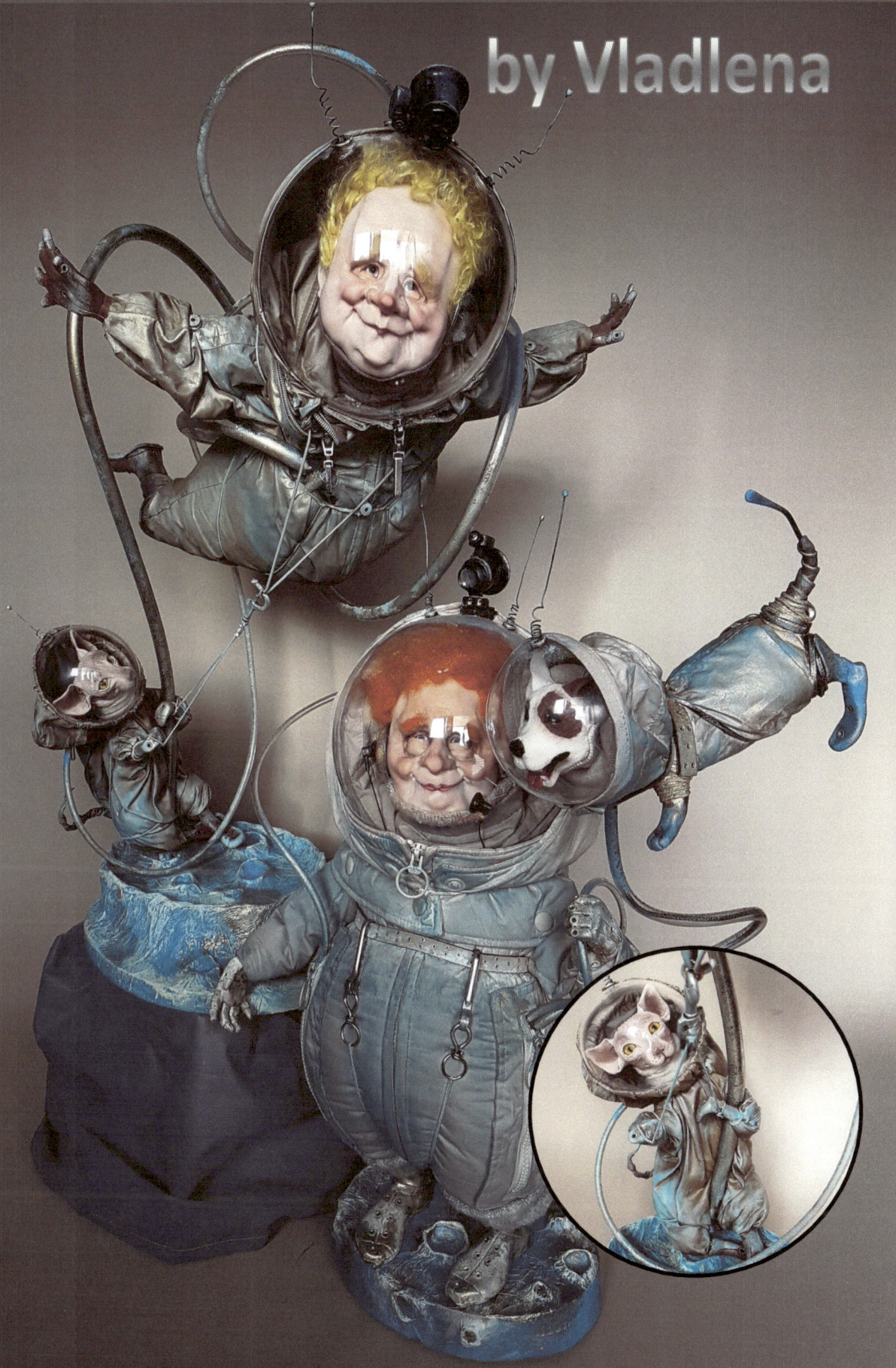

by Vladlena

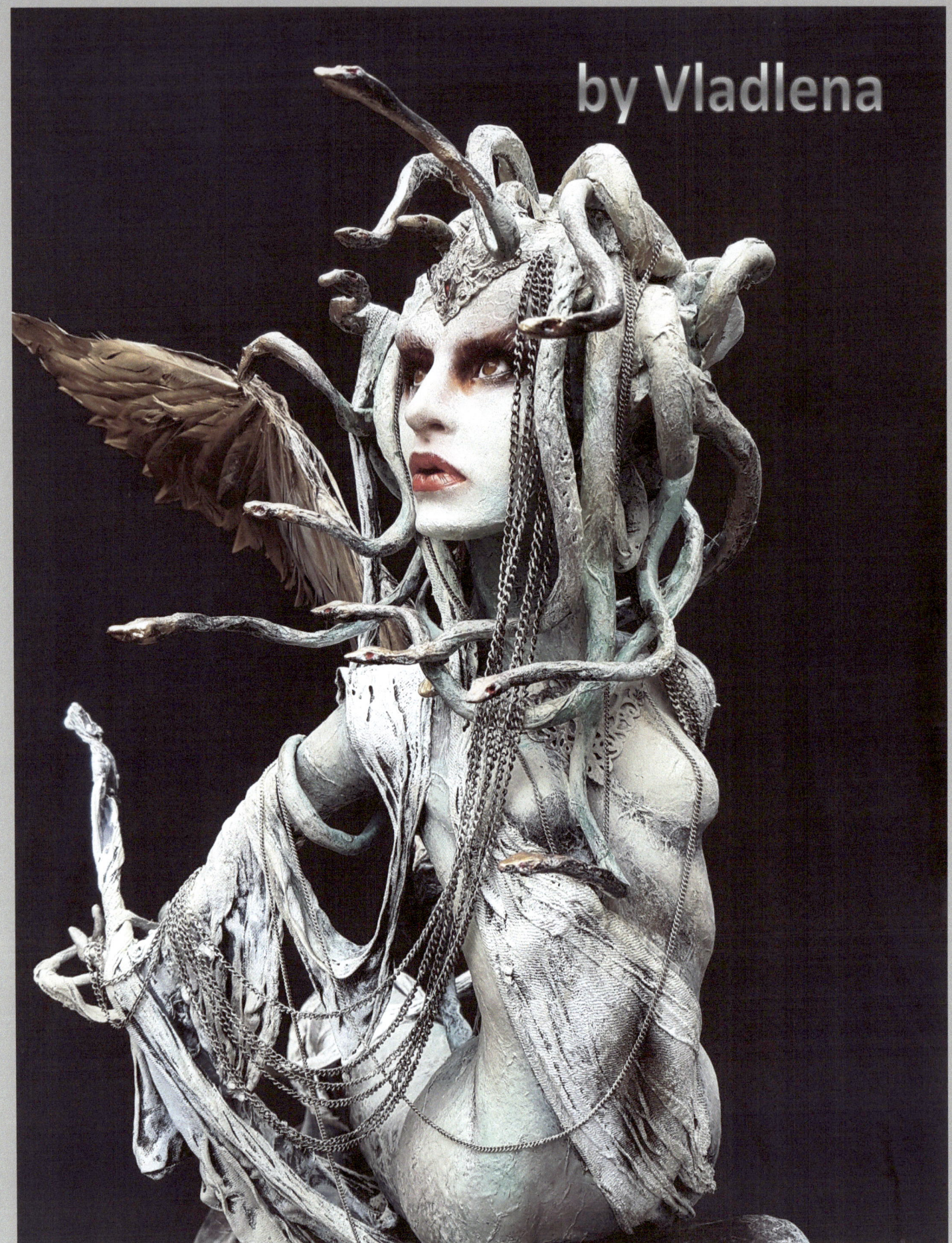

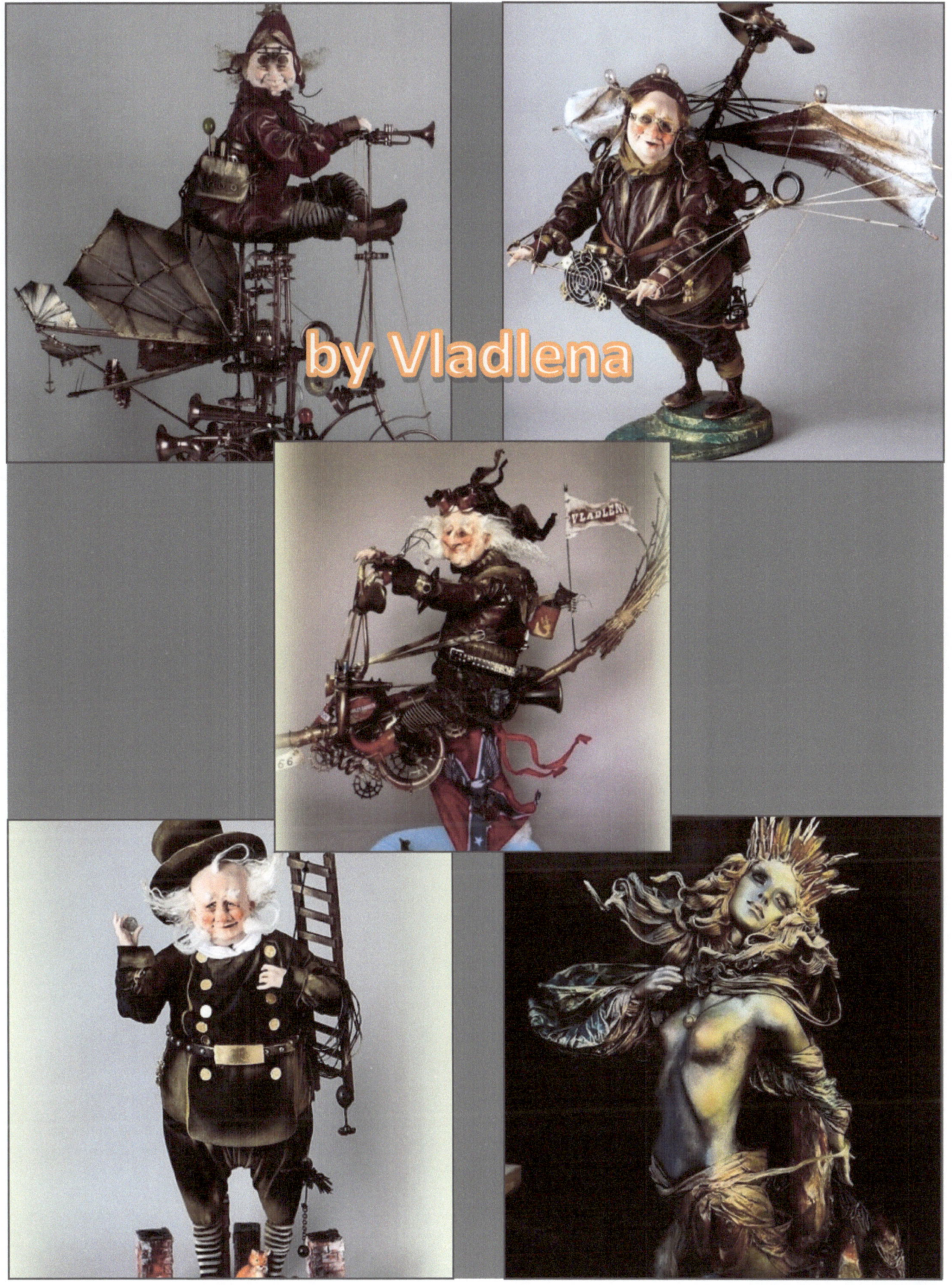

by Vladlena

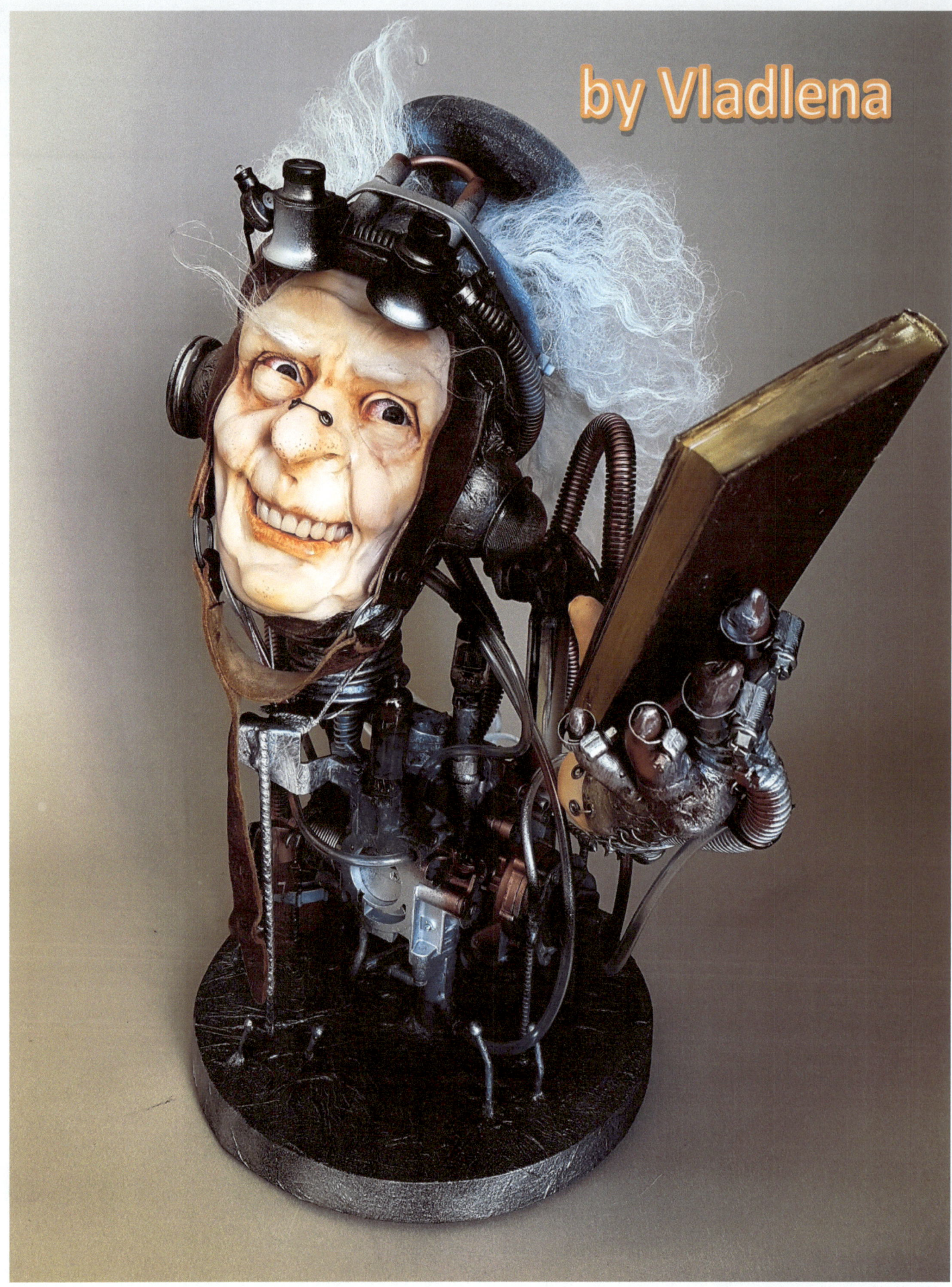

by Vladlena

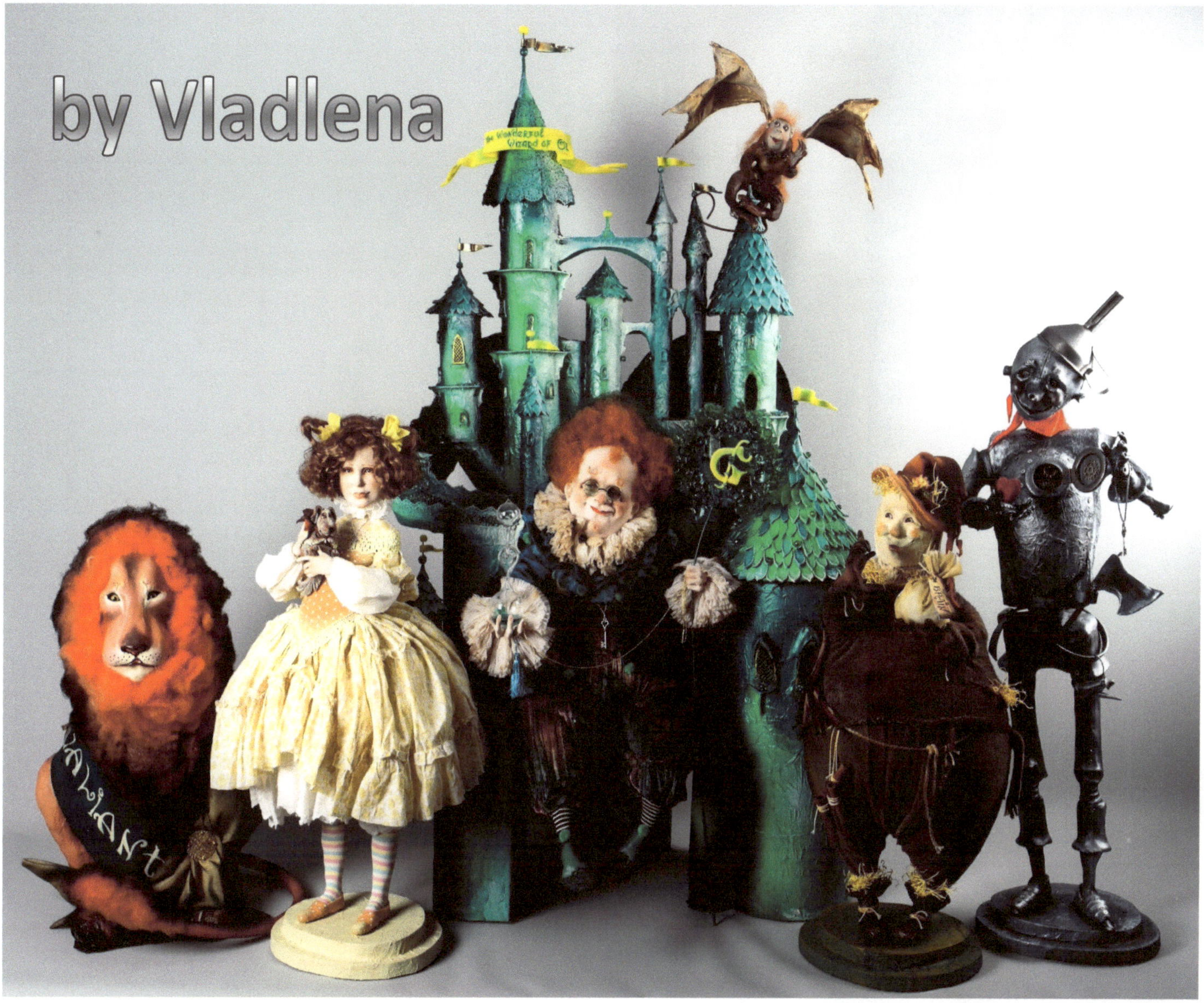

by Vladlena

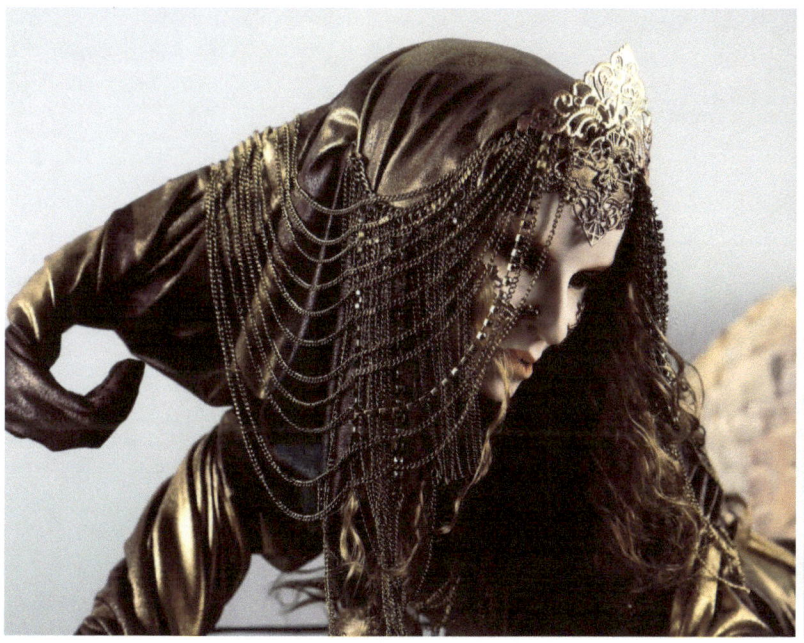
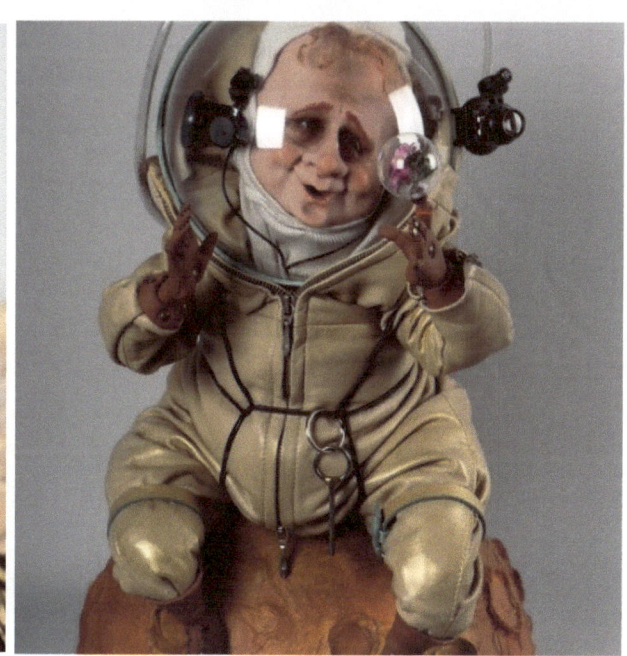

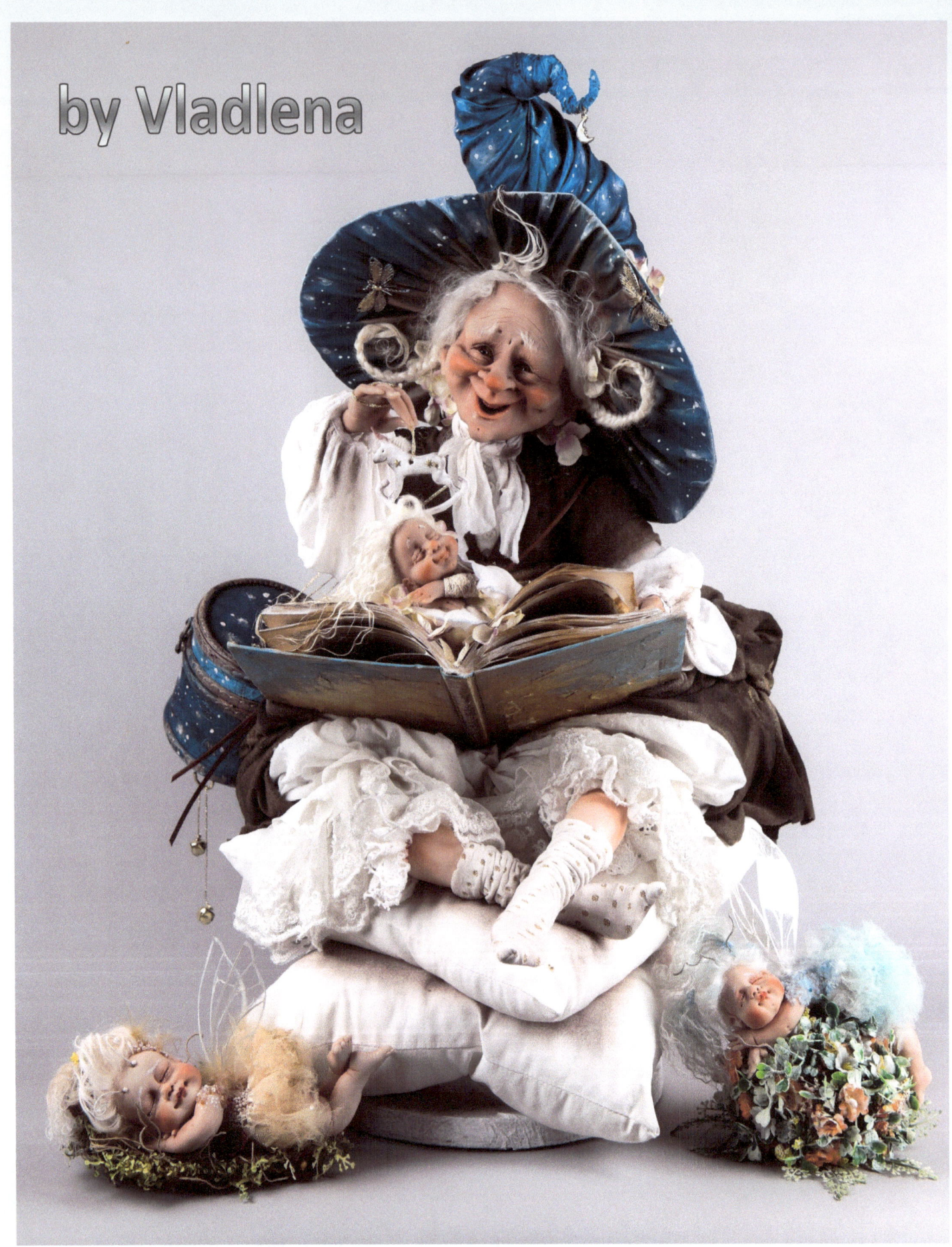

by Vladlena

http://vladlenadoll.com

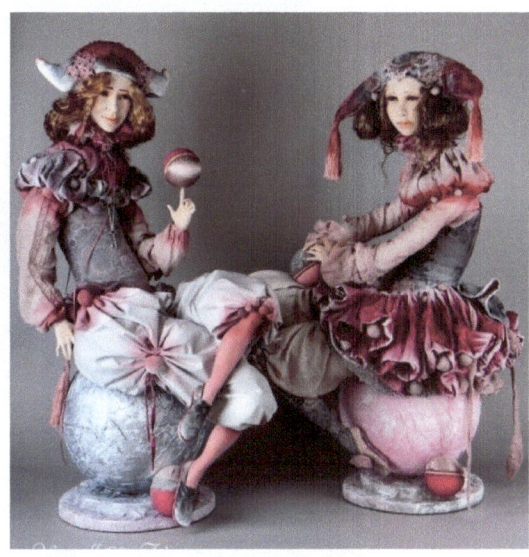
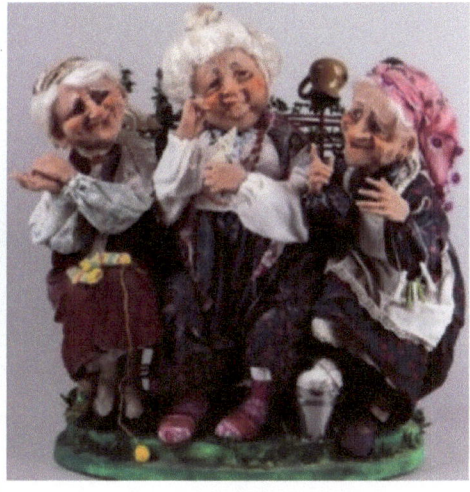
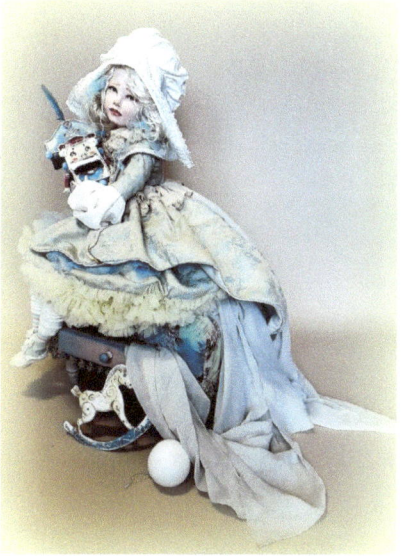
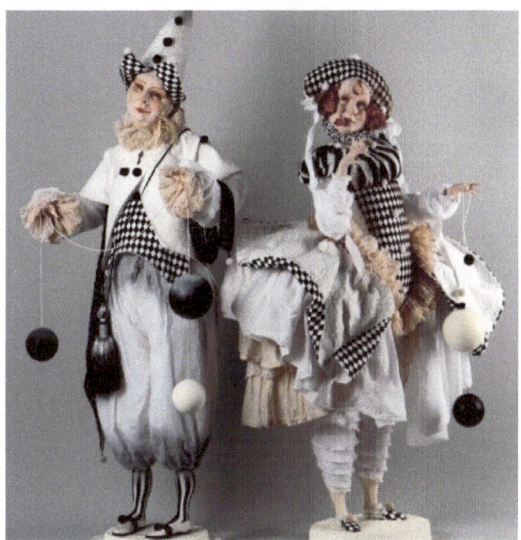
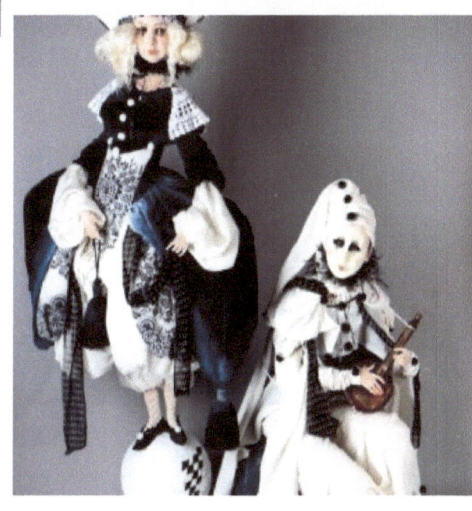
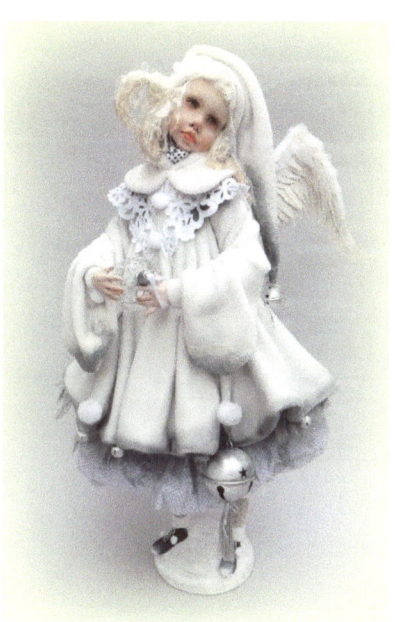

by Vladlena

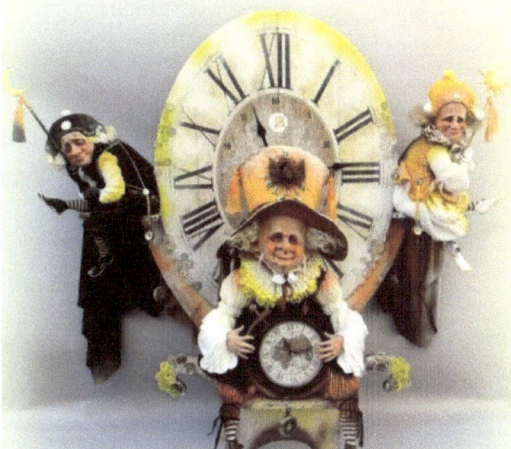
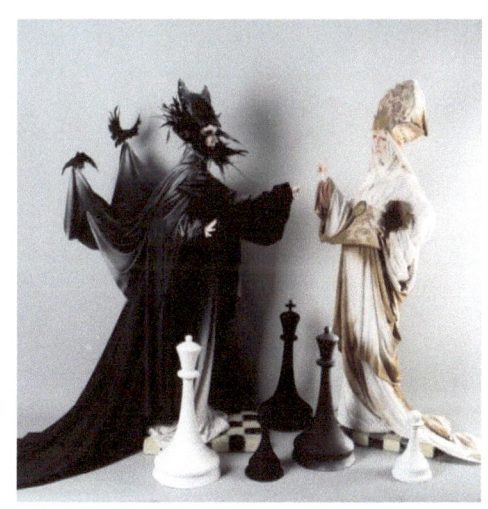
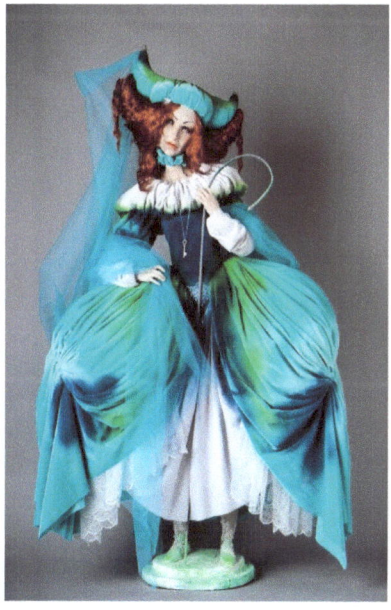

http://vladlenadoll.com

Vladlena's Gallery

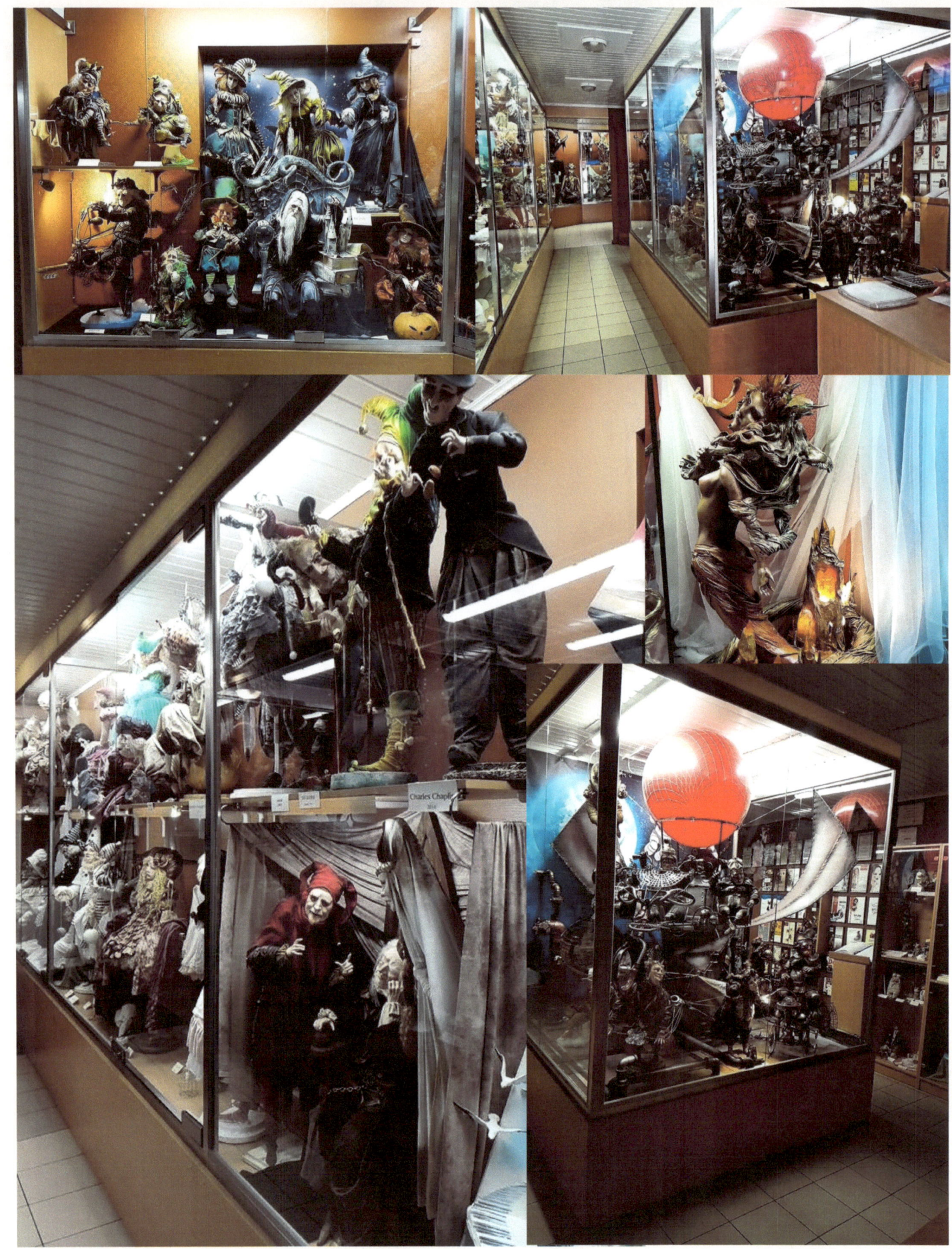

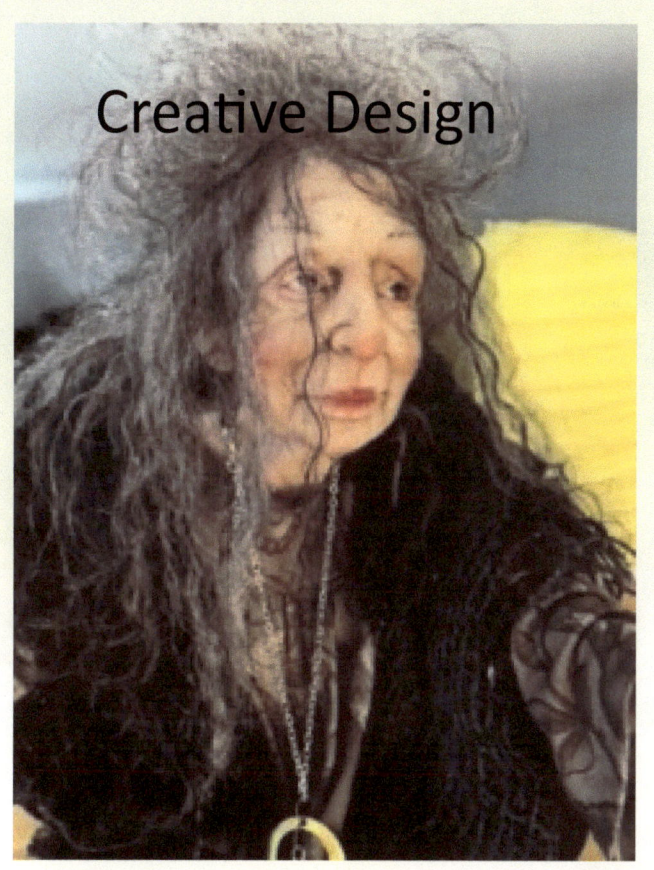

Creative Design

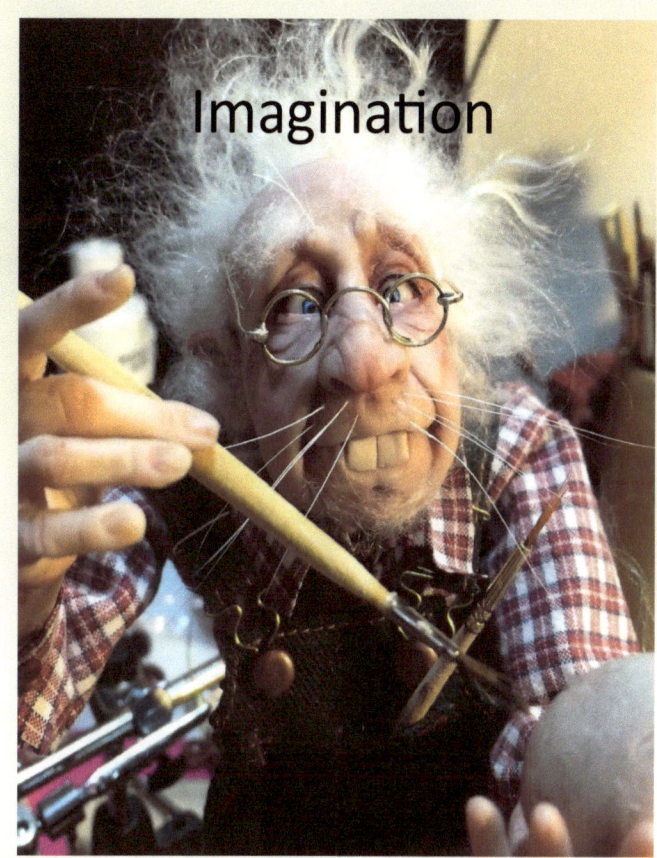

Imagination

Karen Baker

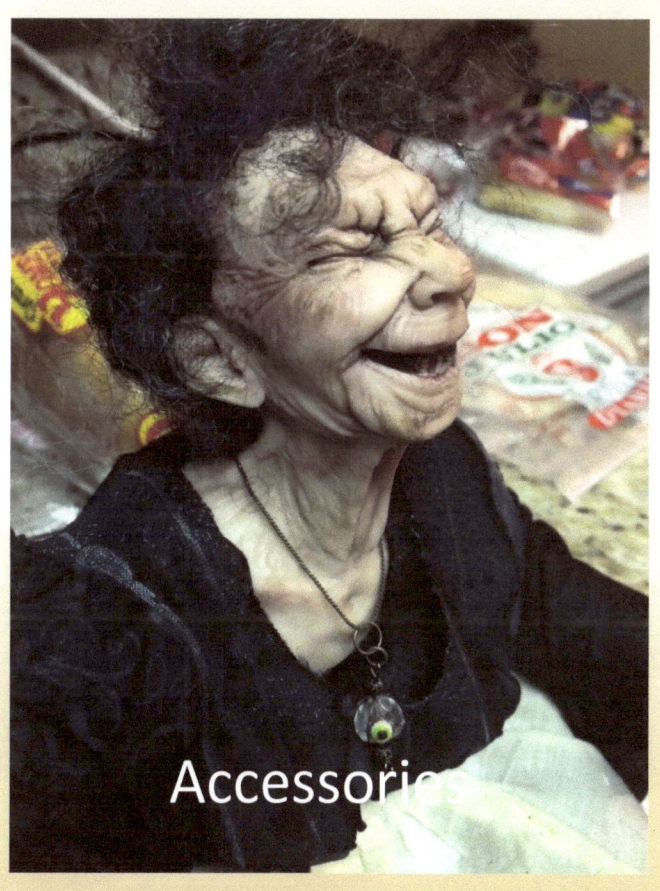

Accessories

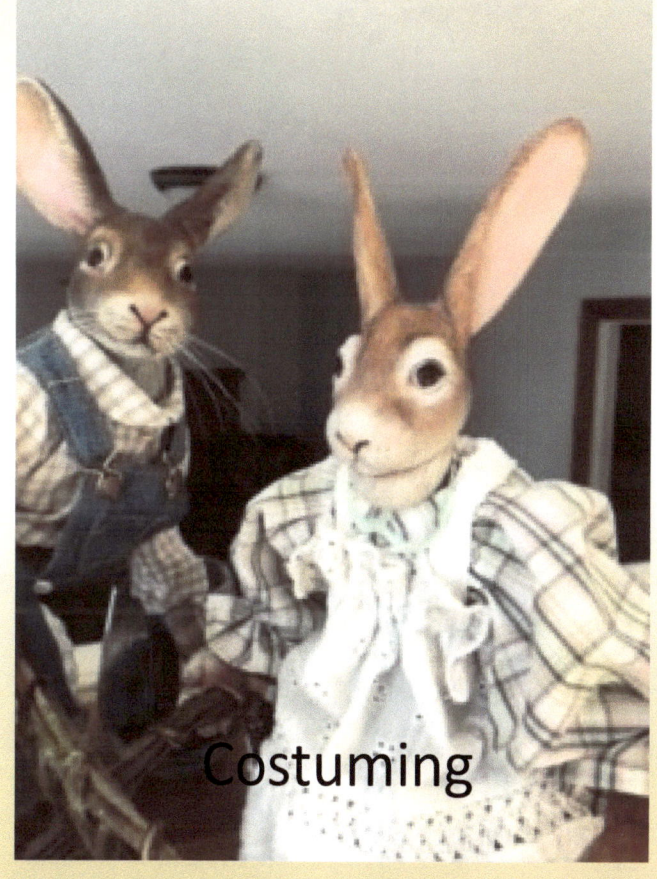

Costuming

karenlovesosa2@gmail.com

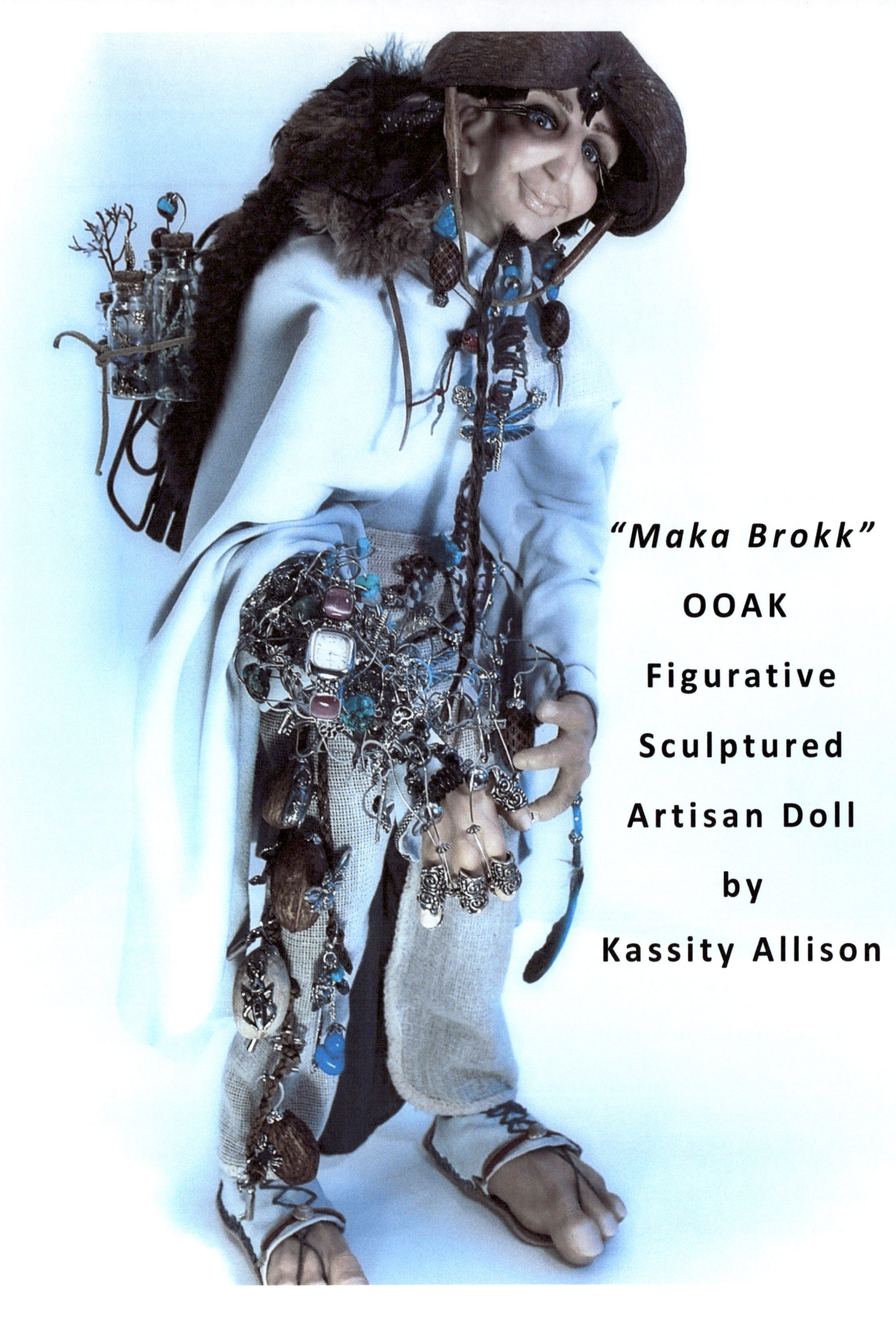

Maka Brokk "Keeper of Time"

Created by Award Winning Artist Kassity Allison

Maka Brokk is a lovable mystical character who not many get to see, for he lives in time itself! He travels from season to season preparing all that will come as each season unfolds and as the days go by. He has a special arm mechanism made of silver, one of earth's precious metals. This arm mechanism carries within it many treasures of stones, gems which grants the keeper to journey through time.

Maka Brokk is an artisan handmade figurative sculpture. He is 24 inches tall with an inner posable armature, which has been created by the artist as an inner skeleton. He then had a fitted cloth body made over the inner skeleton, hand sewn and hand stitched to enhance the body shape.

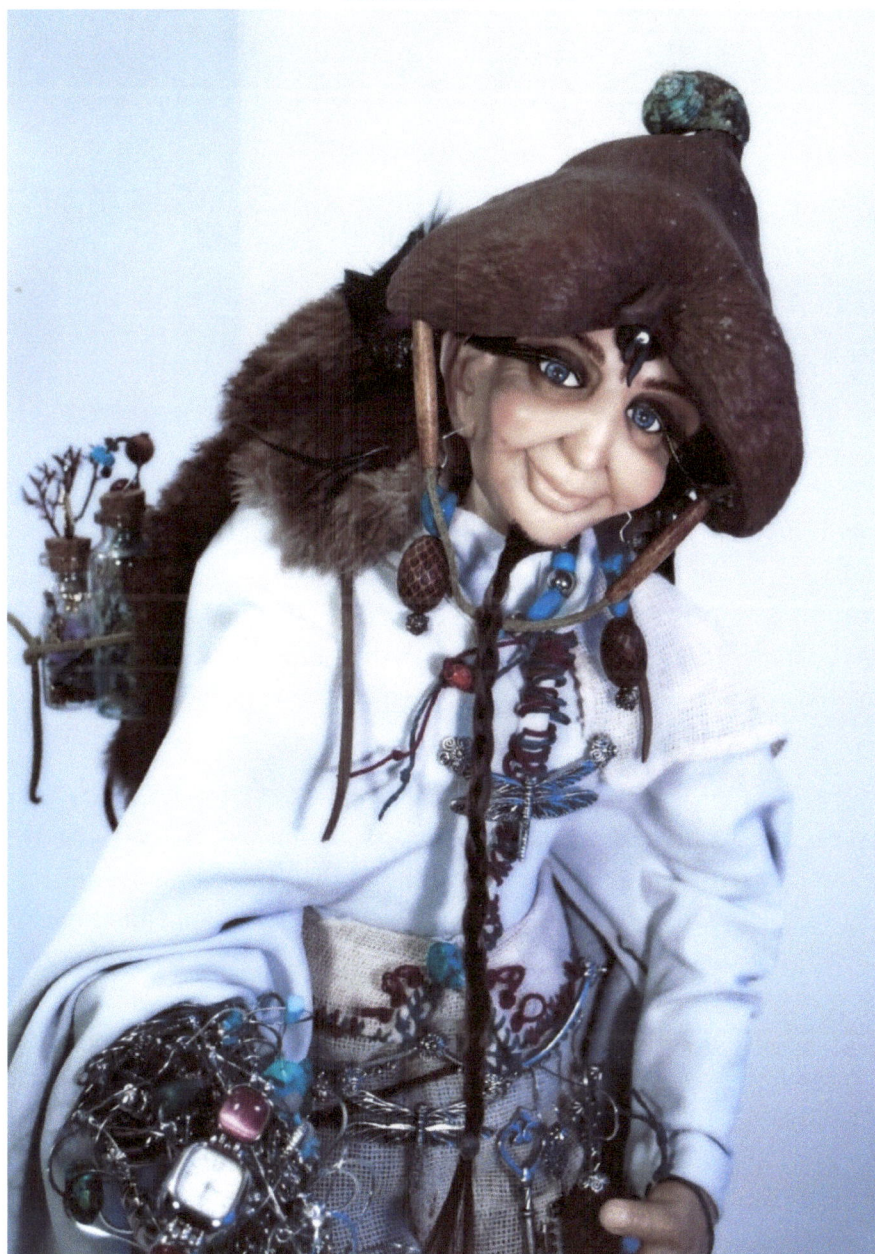

His sculpture parts include his head, hands and feet. He has a soft leather cape with hand stitched trim, and many silver decorative accents, nuts, precious stones. His arm mechanism is handmade from silver with layers of silver designs and precious stones. His pants are made of woven cotton with a fine silk lining. He has handmade leather sandals.

Maka Brokk is finely detailed in every way from his face, hands and feet to the tip of his toes! He has been sculpted out of the best polymer doll clay and carefully baked to ensure a lifelong enjoyment. He has been hand painted by the artist with care; a special layer technique was used to create a life like skin look. His blue eyes are glass; hand painted enhanced by the artist and accented with peacock feathers.

akassity@gmail.com

Accessories are the icing on the cake
Jack Johnston

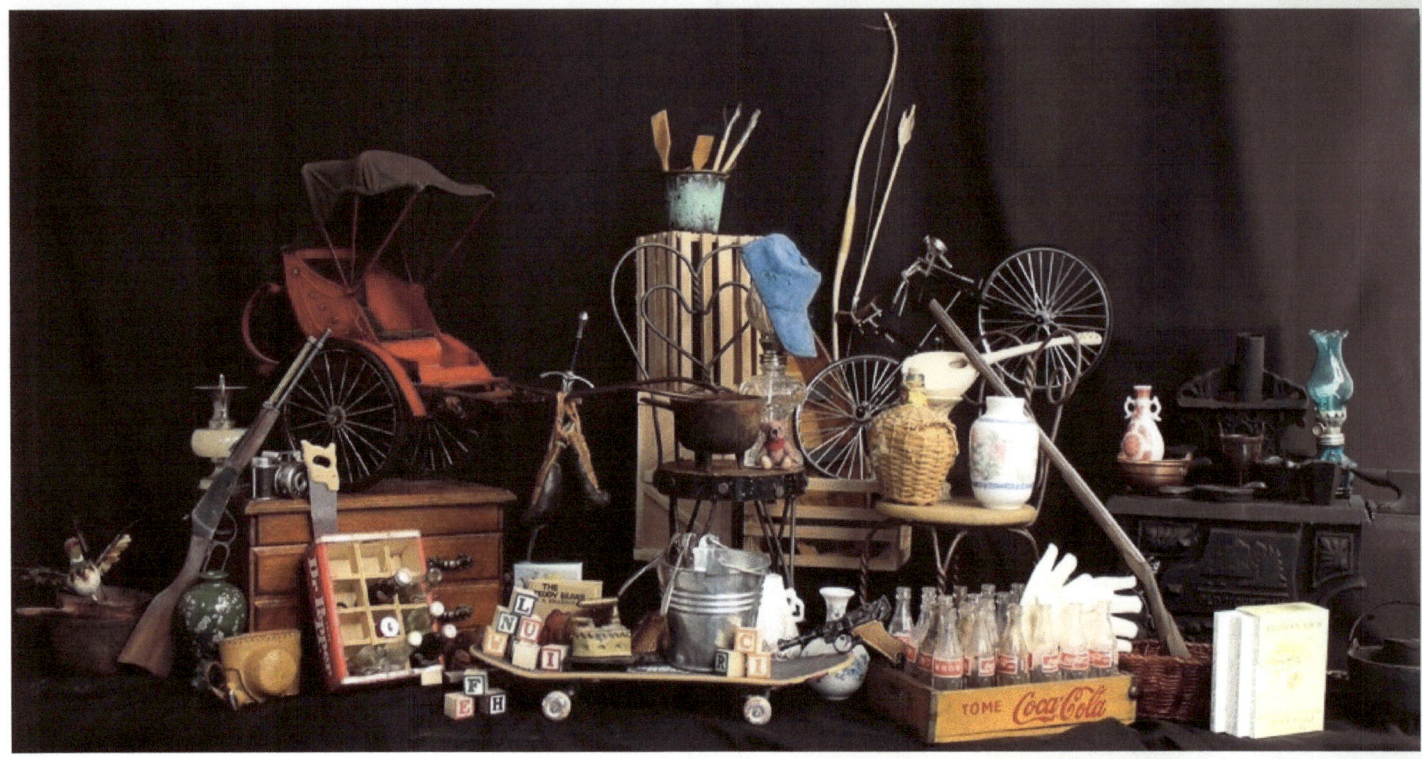

    A sculpture without an accessory is just a sculpture, but a sculpture including a meaningfully placed accessory is an entire story. Think of Norman Rockwell's illustrations; they were rarely just a portrait, they generally included an accessory that helped to tell the complete story. To carry my point to another level, "A photograph is worth a thousand words, but a photograph that includes an accessory allows the viewer to give the story unlimited words.

    To assure that the accessory works with the sculpture there are several things that must be considered and accomplished. First, the accessory should be in the same scale as the sculpture. Secondly, it helps if the accessory is designed in the same genre as the sculpture. For example, If the sculpture is a fantasy character the accessory should also be as fantasy. On the other hand, if the sculpture is realistic, it will enhance the sculpt for the accessory to be realistic too. Keep your eyes open for an accessory for your sculpture as you shop for yourself or for your family. Occasionally I find an accessory in an antique store, toy store or even a garage sale. Using your imagination you can see the accessory used with one of your sculptures in the most unusual way. Notice in the image at the top of this article, I've found everything in miniature from a functioning 35 mm camera (circa 1950) to a full case of Coca Cola bottles (circa 1930). Many of the miniatures shown above were made by life scale manufacturers as salesman samples. In the 30-50's when salesman traveled across the nation selling their goods it was easier to carry a miniature cast iron stove in a brief case than to crate up a full scale sample that could weigh 400 lbs. A salesman could carry a perfectly detailed manufactured chair as a miniature and essentially tell the same story as carrying a life scale chair. These salesman samples are by far the best accessory you will ever find.

I fell in love with the stories that Norman Rockwell told with his imaginative realistic illustrations. As a young man I kept all of the Saturday Evening Post Magazine covers that graced an illustration by Mr. Rockwell. He told more about the character in his illustration with the simple use of accessory than most authors tell in a chapter in their books.

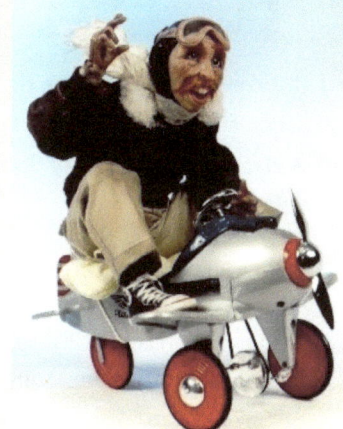

Notice that the "Aviator" that I sculpted in 1996 tells a story about an adult that not only wanted to relive his childhood, but that he wanted to dress up like an aviator and imagine flying while perched on a pedal car that resembled a World War II P-51 fighter. In this case it was my dream as a child to have a pedal car like the one I used in this sculpture. I had always dreamed of flying a P-51 and becoming a fighter pilot. After completing a tour of duty in Vietnam, I finally lived the dream. I used the "GI" bill to pay for certification as a multi-engine aircraft pilot. I become certified to fly all fixed wing aircraft including fighter jets. Now that I'm too old to fly safely, I enjoy looking at my sculpture of the "Aviator". Looking at the images take me back to my childhood and to the years I spent with my hands on the "yoke" of a fighter busting through clouds at 500 mph on my way to fly with the angels.

An accessory does not have to be a full vignette, it can be as simple as one teddy bear, or of course have furniture and accessories on the shelf behind the character to help tell a story. In the vignette of the Teddy Bear Maker below, I built a shelf to go behind the character, a table to go in front of him and scores of teddy bears, to help tell his story. This completed "Vignette" does in fact help tell the story; but look at the simple image of the teddy bear maker holding only one of the teddy bears, it also tells a story.

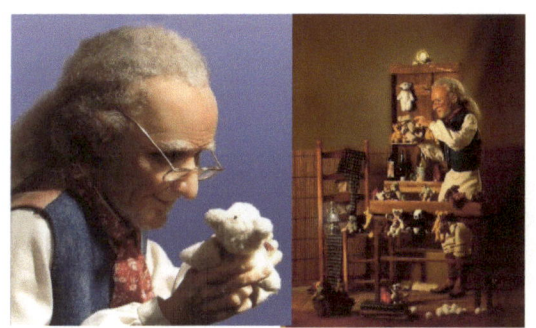

To complement the use of an accessory with a sculpture, make sure the accessory becomes part of the sculpture. Have the character hold the accessory in his or her hands and assure that the character looks at the accessory in a loving and meaningful way. This helps to tell the story much better than just having a teddy bear sitting on his lap or used on a shelf behind him.

Plan the accessory far ahead of sculpting your character. If you can't find an accessory to fit the scale of your sculpture, then sculpt the doll to the scale of the accessory that you've found. There are times that the accessory will become the center of the story instead of the character. In that case you can make the accessory dominant over the sculpted character. To make a very long story short, in the case of promoting my life as a sculptor and a traveling educator, it was simple to use my sculpts and case as accessories.

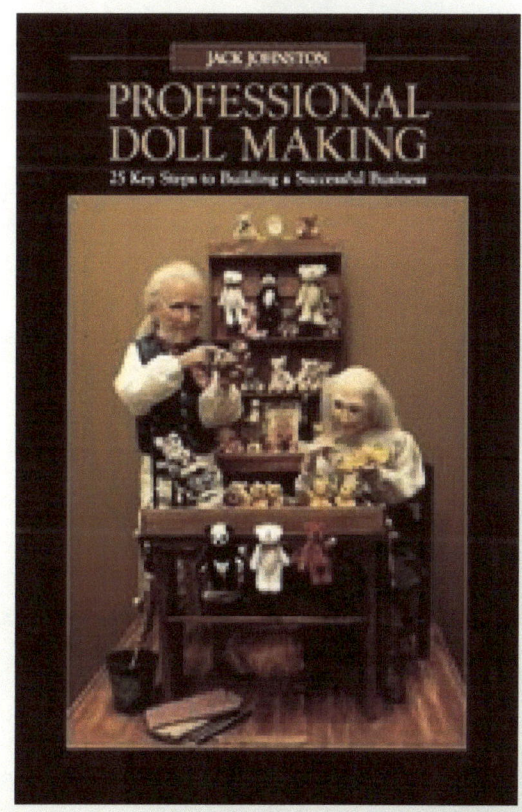

I retired in 2016, but I still enjoy helping my fellow artists with their careers. I've used my retirement time to write another book entitled "Professional Doll Making", 25 ways to build your own doll making business. As always, as members of the Professional Doll Makers Art Guild you are entitled to a 20% discount ($24.95 reduced to $19.95). You may order a personalized copy of my most recent book by calling me at 801-510-3006 or writing me at jjartdolls@gmail.com or clicking on www.artdolls.com.

Elizabetta Visentini

"Accessories are a passion"

The ornaments and how dolls are born from the accessories. In each of my creations I try to add details and small accessories that make everything as complete as possible. The accessories are the thing that make my work come alive, complete, and I really enjoy making them. The decoration, finishing and detail phase is the one that allows me to give more space to the imagination. Accessories are a passion. They can be bows, jewels, ornaments or real instruments of the character. I like to make different types of sculptures and this allows me to create unique details every time with special value. It may even happen that around the idea of an accessory the whole doll is born. It happens to me very often. If I create a steampunk lady I can indulge in the realization of everything that can embellish her, creating a fashion outfit complete with scepter, hat and details on the dress. If instead I decide to make an ogre or a monster, I can have fun creating weapons, tools or horrid details to make the scene more truthful. When I make eggs and I want to give them a precise connotation,

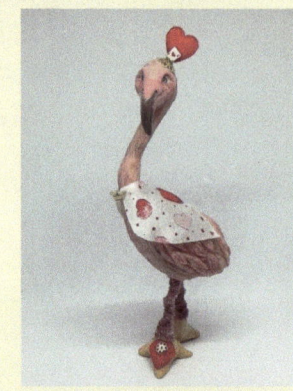

I often focus on a detail. Very characteristic of the subject: as for example the beer mug for the Leprechaun egg, or the piercings for the punk egg...sometimes a simple accessory can give a lot of identity, especially for these easy characters.

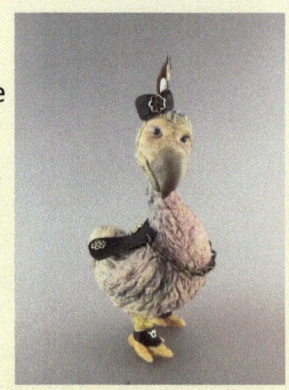

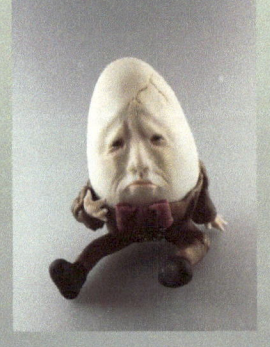

I love making these tools entirely by hand, if possible. Or decorating miniatures of pre-existing objects. I particularly like to make small jewels in metallic wire and micro beads that can become necklaces, crowns or more complex structures. For these realizations I draw on small metal parts that are usually used for jewels. I love making small caps in polymer clay, in the style of the Mad Hatter, very decorative and nice. I like to use trimmings and materials from different uses. I often collect particular natural elements during the holidays to always create new and original things.

I am organizing myself to be able to use fluid metals and particular rein to have more and more accurate, original and precious result to make my works unique and recognizable. In the last work, which are poseable dolls, I have introduced the possibility of being able to change accessories, in such a way as to be able to interact more with the doll, which becomes a living sculpture, with which to have a more playful. My desire is to create ooak that can establish a relationship with the collector. That can be watched, that you can enjoy their presence and have a strong feeling with their presence, thanks to the accessories, which certainly make the difference.

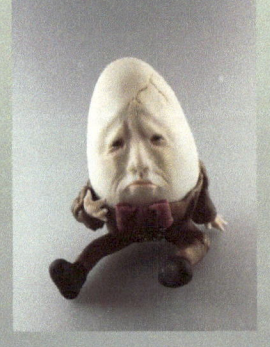
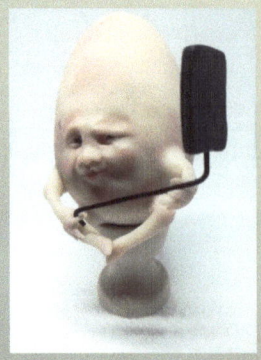
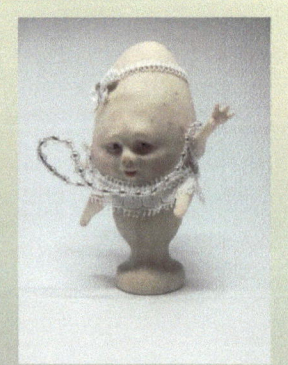
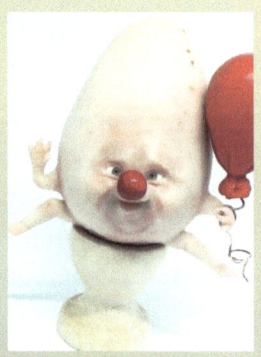

elisabetta.visentini@gmail.com

Elizabetta Visentini

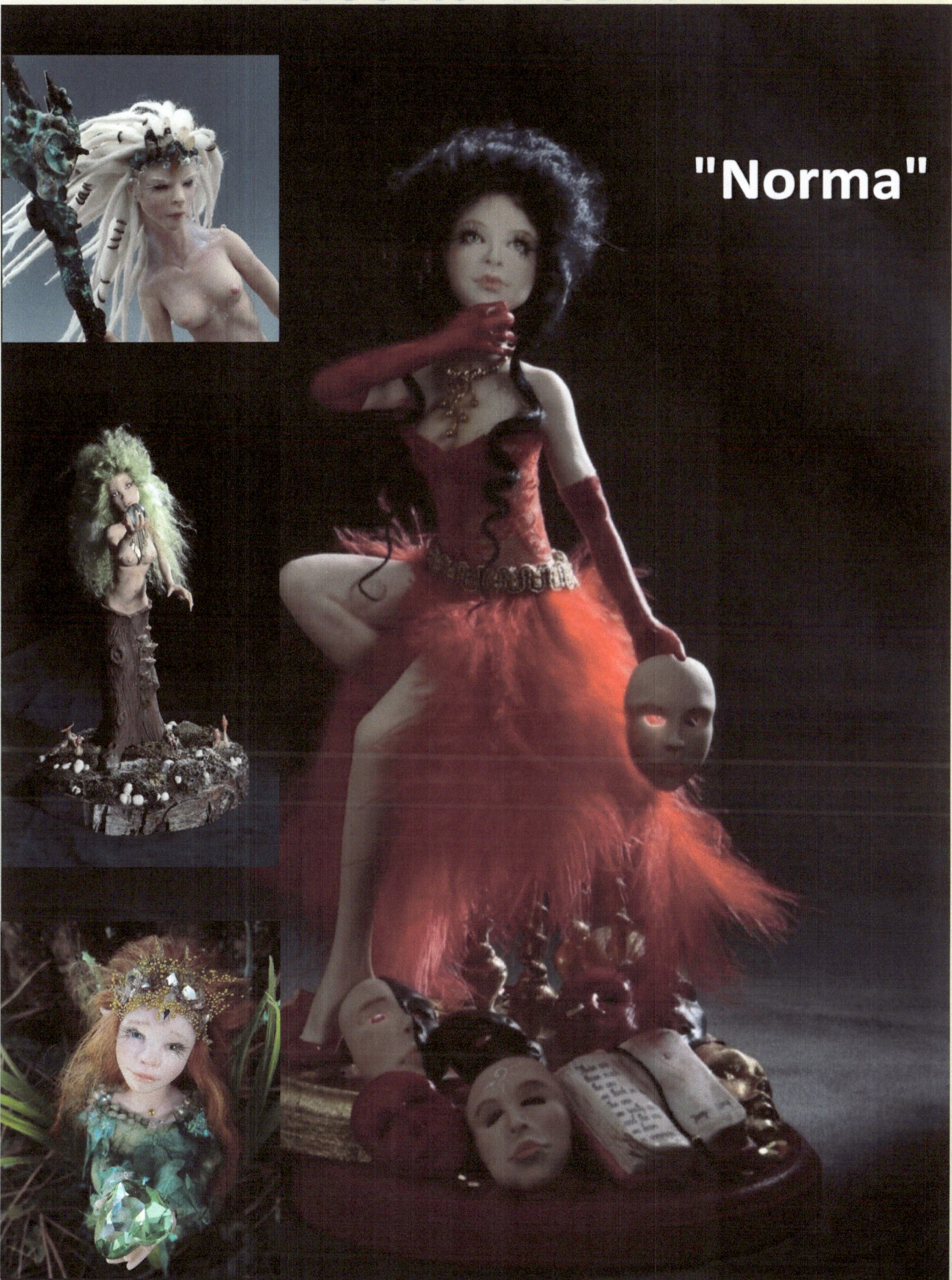

"Norma"

Making a DOLL PURSE

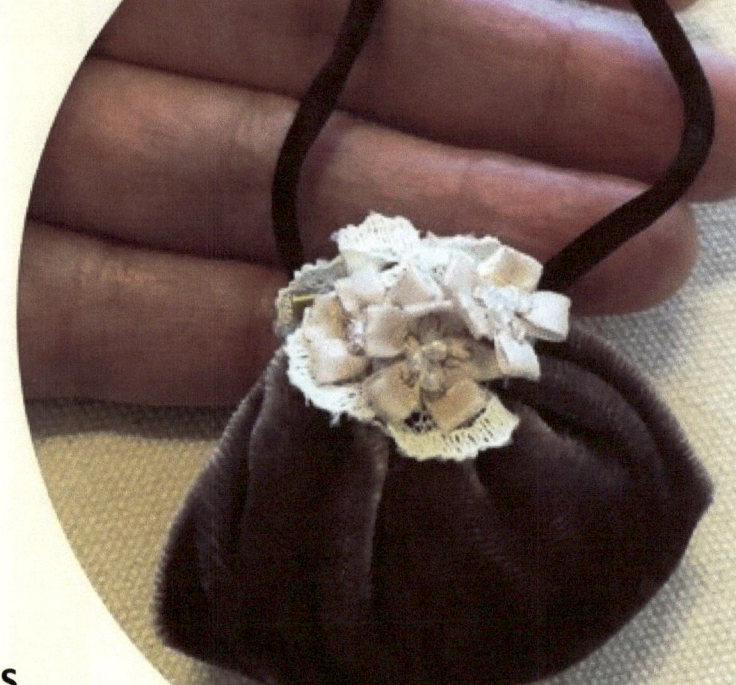

SUPPLIES

4.25" square of fabric

6" Soutache Cord

6" piece of 1/4" flat scalloped lace

6 tiny flowers or any embellishments

Ribbon Crimp

Small Ball of Fiberfill

Sewing Needle

Matching Thread

Straight Pins

Scissors

Fabric Glue

Padded Pliers

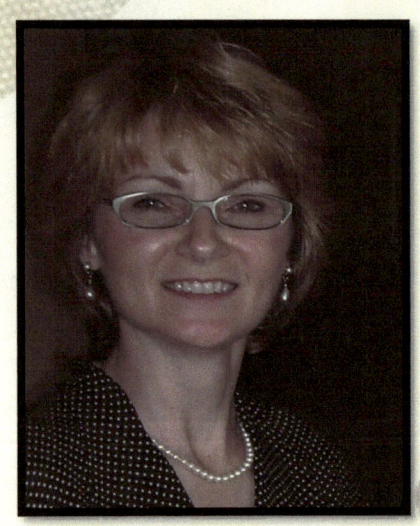

By

Lisa Wroblewski

cecilandcousa@yahoo.com

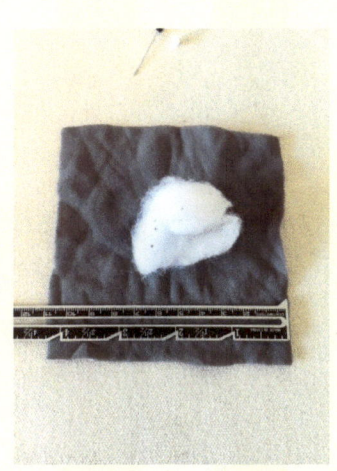 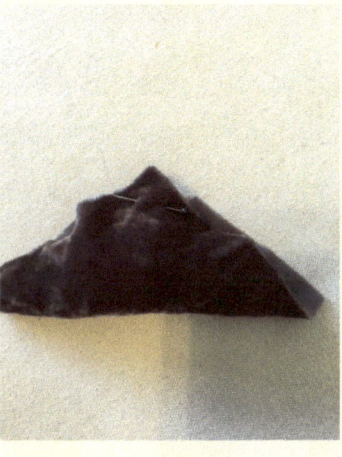 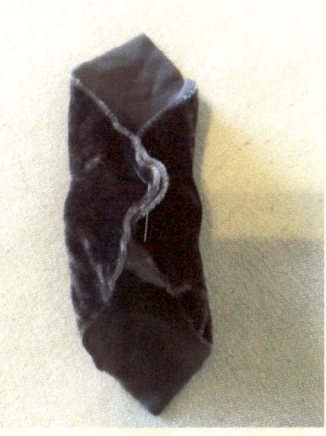 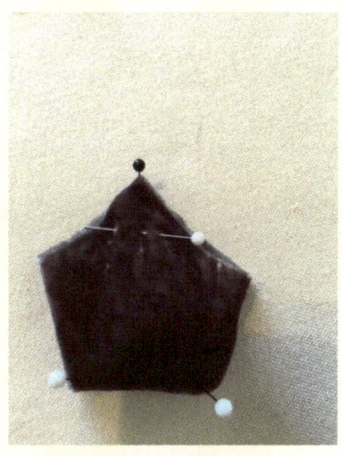

Lay your fabric square with the wrong side up and place a small amount of fiberfill in the center. Fold one corner on top of the opposite corner and pin. Place a bit of glue between the fabric just under the pin to tack your fabric in place then trim off excess corner fabric. Lay your fabric so that the corners that are glued are facing up. Pin the opposite corners together. On a padded surface place pins at the bottom to hold it's shape.

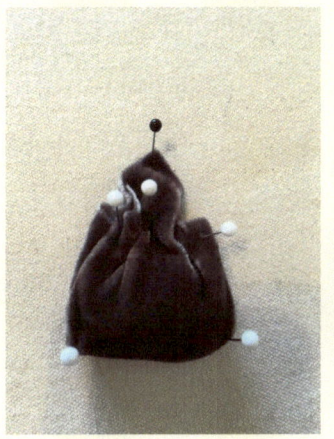 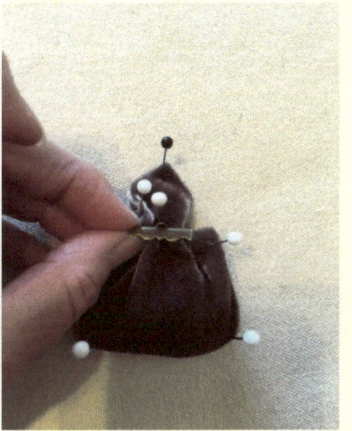 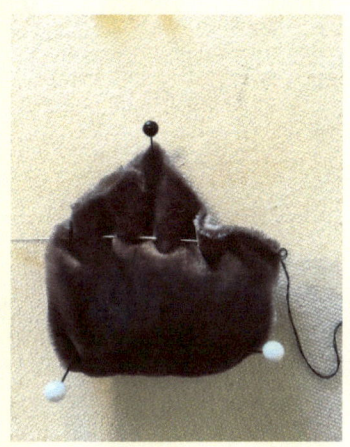 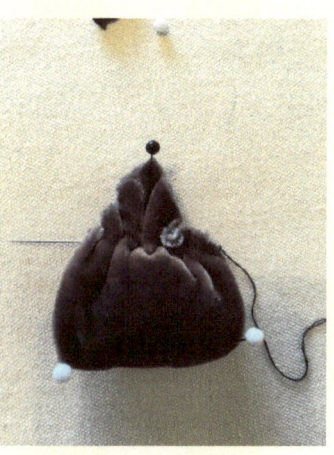

Place pins at the top sides to hold your purse shape as you determine the correct size for gathering the top. Check the width of your top to ensure it will fit under the ribbon crimp. Thread a hand sewing needle with matching thread and knot one end. Using a running stitch gather the fabric near the top where the crimp will be attached. Knot off to secure.

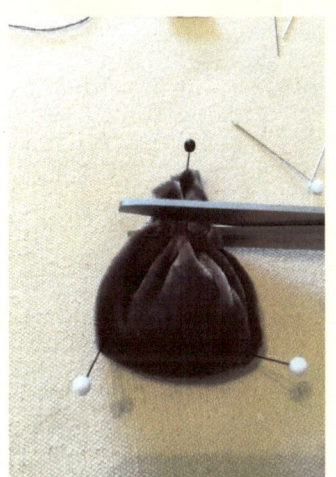 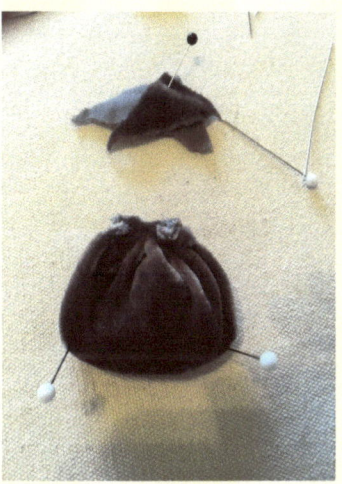 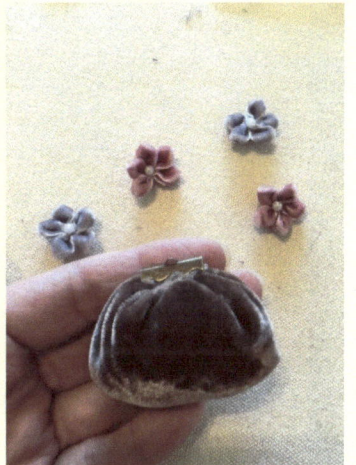 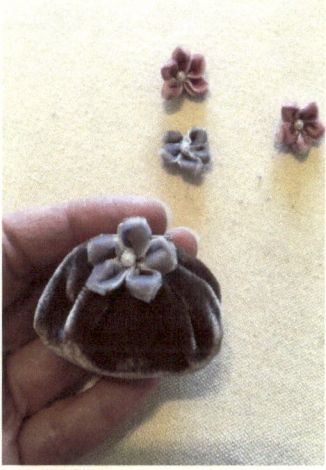

Place the ribbon crimp over your gathered stitches to know where to trim off the excess fabric. Trim off excess fabric at the top. Once your fabric is gathered to size, open the ribbon crimp enough to insert the top gathered fabric. If you do not have padded pliers use regular pliers with a cloth to prevent making marks on your ribbon crimp. Clamp your ribbon crimp onto your purse top hiding the raw edges. Embellish with flowers, beads, lace or whatever you wish.

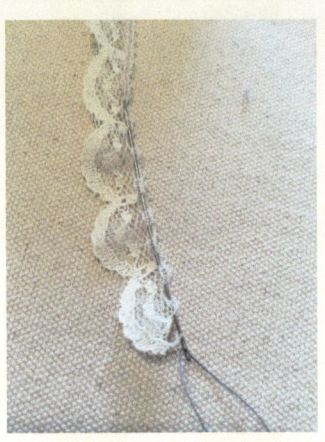 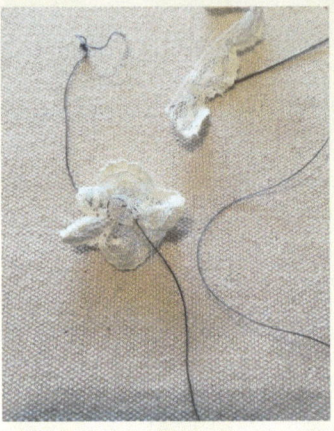 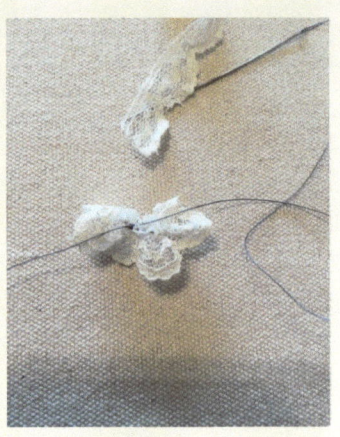 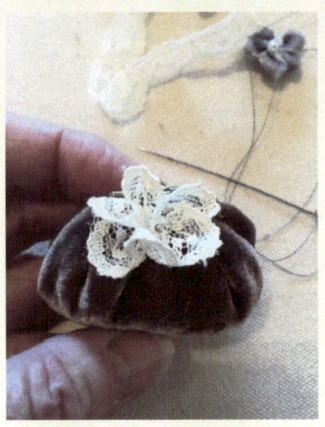

To create a lace flower, take approximately 6" of a 1/4" flat scalloped lace and hand sew a running stitch all the way to the end. Pull your thread to gather your lace into a nice rosette. Knot off the thread to secure. Sew or glue onto the top of your mini purse.

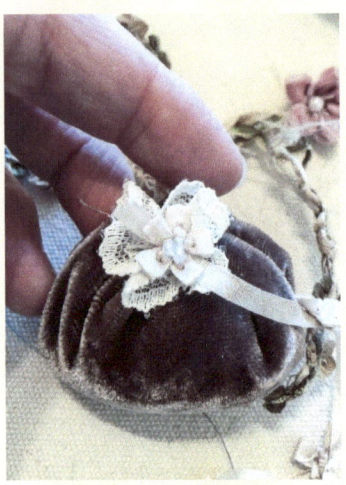 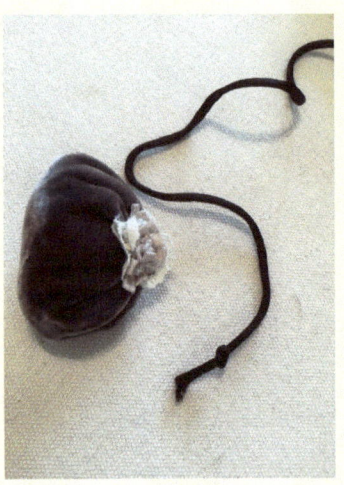 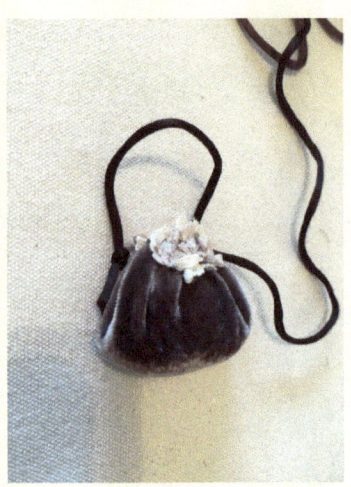 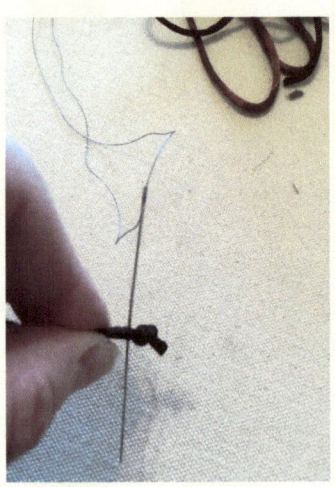

Once your lace rosette is attached you can adorn it with tiny beads, flowers or any other embellishments you wish. To add the handle, take approximately 6" of cord and knot one end. Hold the cord up to the purse to determine what length handle you would like. Add a knot at the end and trim excess. Sew through the cord right above the knot.

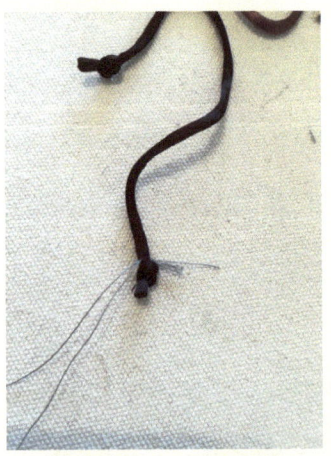 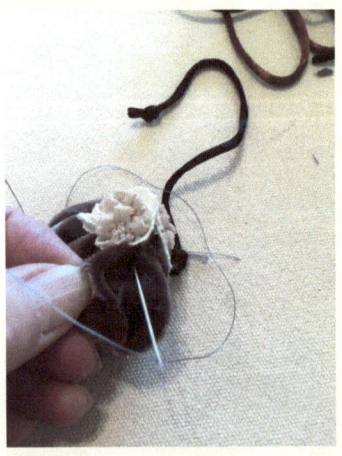 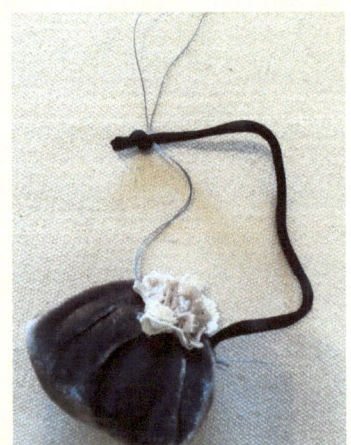 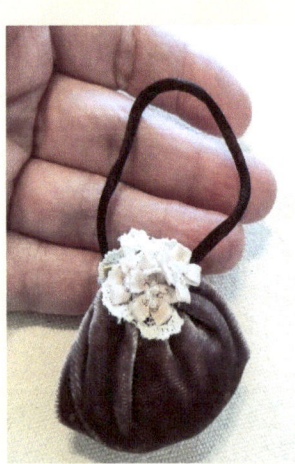

While your needle is still attached to the cord, place the needle into one side of the purse and draw your thread all the way through to exit the other side. Then sew through the knot at the other end of the cord and knot off to secure your handle. Your tiny doll purse is all ready to accessorize your favorite doll.

Lindsey Jones

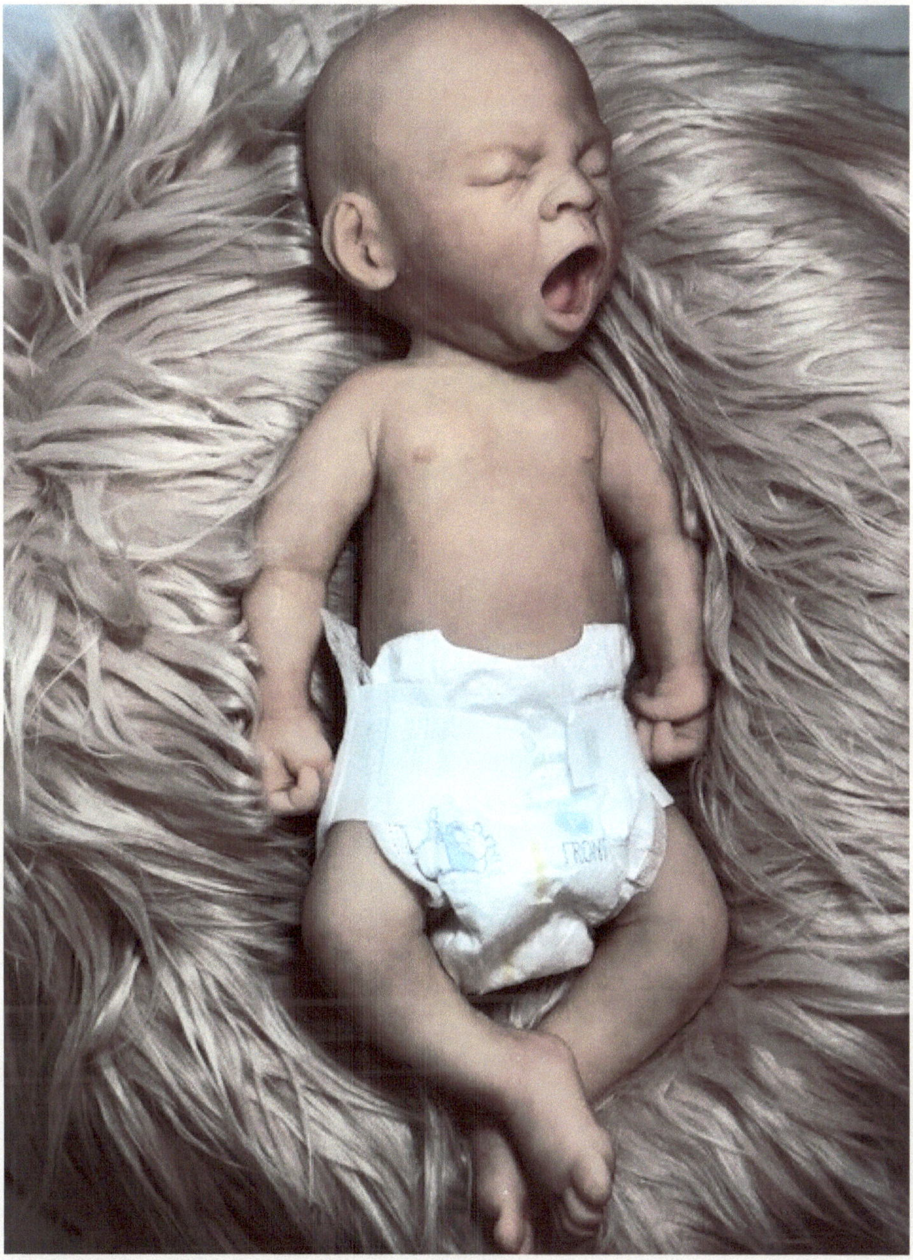

presents...
"Piper"

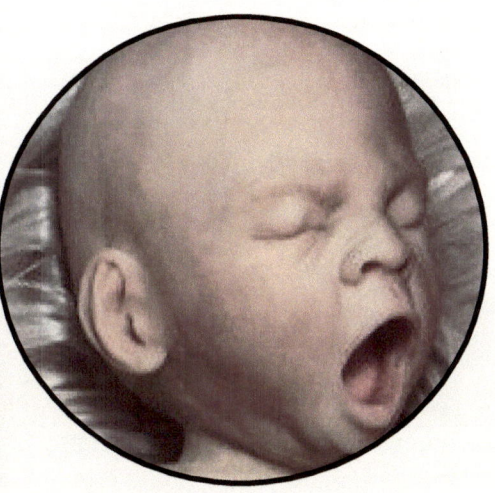

Piper is a full body silicone doll created by artist Lindsey Jones. Lindsey has been sculpting for just under two years with the help of her mentor, Maisa Said. And while she is a beginner, her talents and techniques are continually improving. While learning to sculpt Lindsey is also learning the art of silicone mold making to cast her clay sculpts. Once the cast is complete she then uses silicone paints to bring her babies to life. The final touch is micro rooting the hair one to two hairs a time for added realism.

You can follow her work, view progress photos, and see available babies on her Facebook page "Creations by Lindsey."

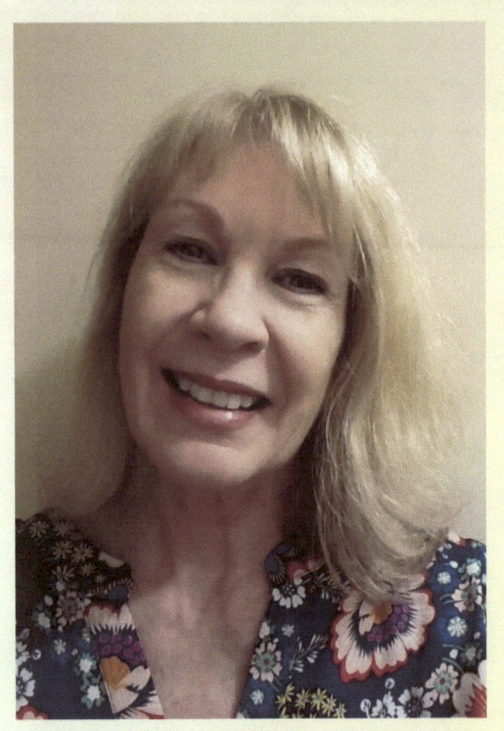

Using Accessories to Inspire, Inspiration to Accessorize!
By Leann Marshall

Throughout the six years I've concentrated on sculpting OOAK art dolls, I've never considered costuming, accessorizing or even design to be my strong points. When I first began seriously sculpting figures over wire armatures, the sculpting itself was my main focus. I wanted to identify my weak points and study how to overcome them one by one. Everything else was more or less afterthought. That was fine for then, but I came to realize that costume and accessories and design ARE ALL part of the finished figure, and each plays a huge part in its success for failure as an art piece.

So just what is an accessory anyway? It's defined as a "thing that can be added to something else in order to make it more useful, versatile, or attractive." Focusing on the third one seems most to our purpose when creating a finished figure, and attractiveness doesn't only mean "beauty," but "appeal." These two things are very subjective, and what one person finds attractive may be totally opposite of what another person likes. But while this may be true, there are a few basic thoughts to keep in mind as far as making everything work together.

Even now I find the whole business of costuming a challenge, multi-layered in complexities. For example, while I very much admire simplicity in color and form, I do admire rich beading, sparkling gems and glitter, and the use of gorgeous hand-dyed fabrics. And while I love natural touches, I also adore utilization of things found in secondhand stores and re-purposed items that have been altered to enhance a figure or its base. And that's an important point to make—that whatever the technique chosen, simple or exotic, the whole idea should be to enhance the figure and pull it all together, not cover it up.

Extreme detail *can* be simple, as in monochromatic costumes. For example, if all the beads and fabrics and lace are white, it can be dazzling but not overcome the actual figure. A more simple monochrome can also be very dramatic, while vibrant colors can actually convey a message about your piece and stir emotions. As long as there is some sense of design to bring it all together and is as a whole pleasing to the eye, the possibilities really are endless. Two very different commissioned dolls illustrate this:

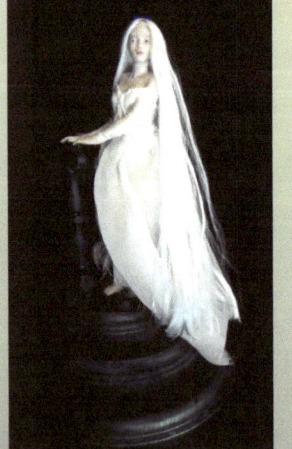

The first is a small monochromatic young ghost lady in white standing atop some stairs I made from wood and cardboard, which I painted black. The resulting contrast is dramatic. PHOTO 1

The other was created for a customer who was very specific about everything. The doll was to be a mermaid with wings, and the colors were to be gold and a bold cerulean blue. I was skeptical about combining them at first and I'm sure it would have never to occurred to me to do so on my own, but then I decided to pull the two colors together with a beaded head dress that used both, and somehow it seemed to work.. PHOTO 2

www.leannmarshall.com

There are times we all lack inspiration. Your muse is on extended vacation and your mind seems like one big blank. Slow down. Time spent thinking and feeling and planning is more important than I ever wanted to admit, because I can be very impatient. While there's something to be said for being spontaneous, an at least partially formed idea of what you will be creating is very helpful and carries noticeably through into your work. If you like to sketch, sit down and make several of them. (I'm too impatient to do that!) If an idea pops into your head write it down a.s.a.p. Make a list of trinkets, objects and fabrics and see where brainstorming takes you. I actually love to make lists, because just the simple act of doing so helps stir up ideas. And as I'm sure you already know, music can inspire feelings that carry over into your art and manifest through color, message, attitude, and passion. You can be serious about your art, still have fun, and not fall into a rut.

And while it's common to feel a creative block when thinking about dressing and a accessorizing your next figure, that's okay. More than okay, because inspiration is everywhere—books, magazines, the internet, and taking a walk in nature's beauty or through an eclectic shop. While I often sculpt the figure first and go from there, more often than not I create the doll with something already in mind and inspired by something I have seen or already acquired. And object can absolutely be an inspiration, such as an unusual seashell or a lovely bit of fine lace. I acquired a small, well-loved wicker doll chair that inspired a woman relaxing at her beach house.

PHOTO 3   Feathers inspired an unusual mermaid tail,
                PHOTO 4

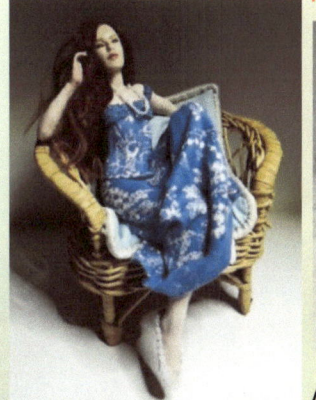 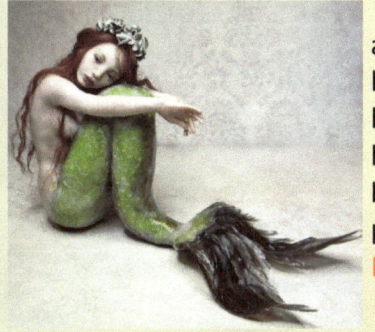 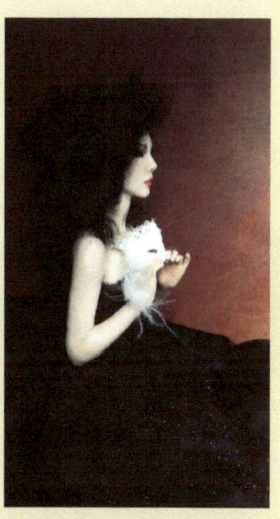

and a woman ready for a costume ball holds a mask I made from a tiny bit of beautiful fine lace, micro beads and a hint of feather—the little mask actually became the focal point of the whole piece.
PHOTO 5

A string of beautiful little shells inspired a shell baby, PHOTO 6
While a larger shell became a little fairy girl's playtime pal. PHOTO 7
A string of hearts became center stage for a Valentine theme. PHOTO 8

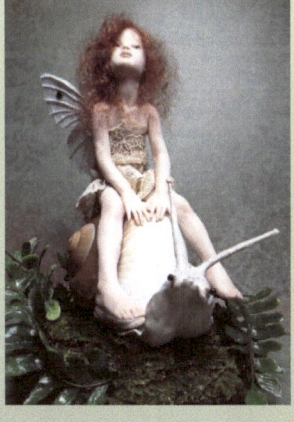 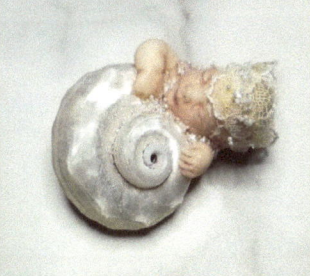 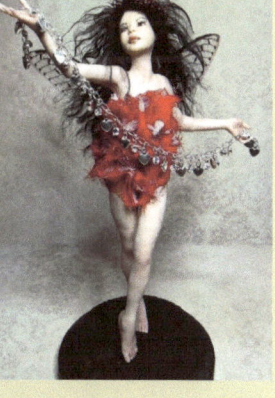

Take advantage of other artistic endeavors you can employ. Accessories don't have to be sought and bought! Utilize some materials you already have and make something yourself. Recently, various D.I.Y. articles on how to make flowers from paper stirred my interest in making my own faux dried flower petals and a small yellow flower—which then inspire my fairy, Isla. She also wears a skirt I fashioned from part of a scarf.

PHOTO 9 If you begin to dress and accessorize a figure and something doesn't seem to "fit" in with it, pay attention to the thoughts playing around in the back of your head and start again. Surround yourself with your stash of materials and hold them up to the figure. Play with what you have, and something that you've had sitting around of a shelf for a long time might turn into just the thing that inspires—that pulls everything together! That has happened to me many times, and it's always a surprise. Take the time to experiment!! Most of all, keep your imagination alive and your creative soul always open to new things!

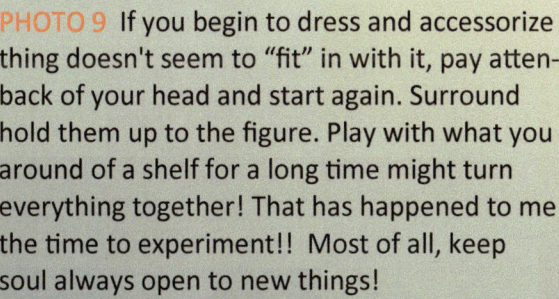 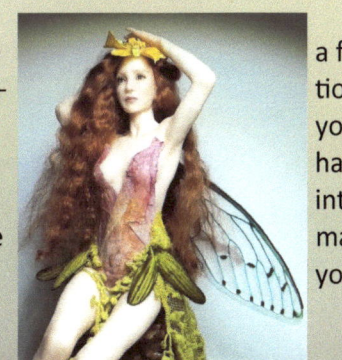

Leann Marshall

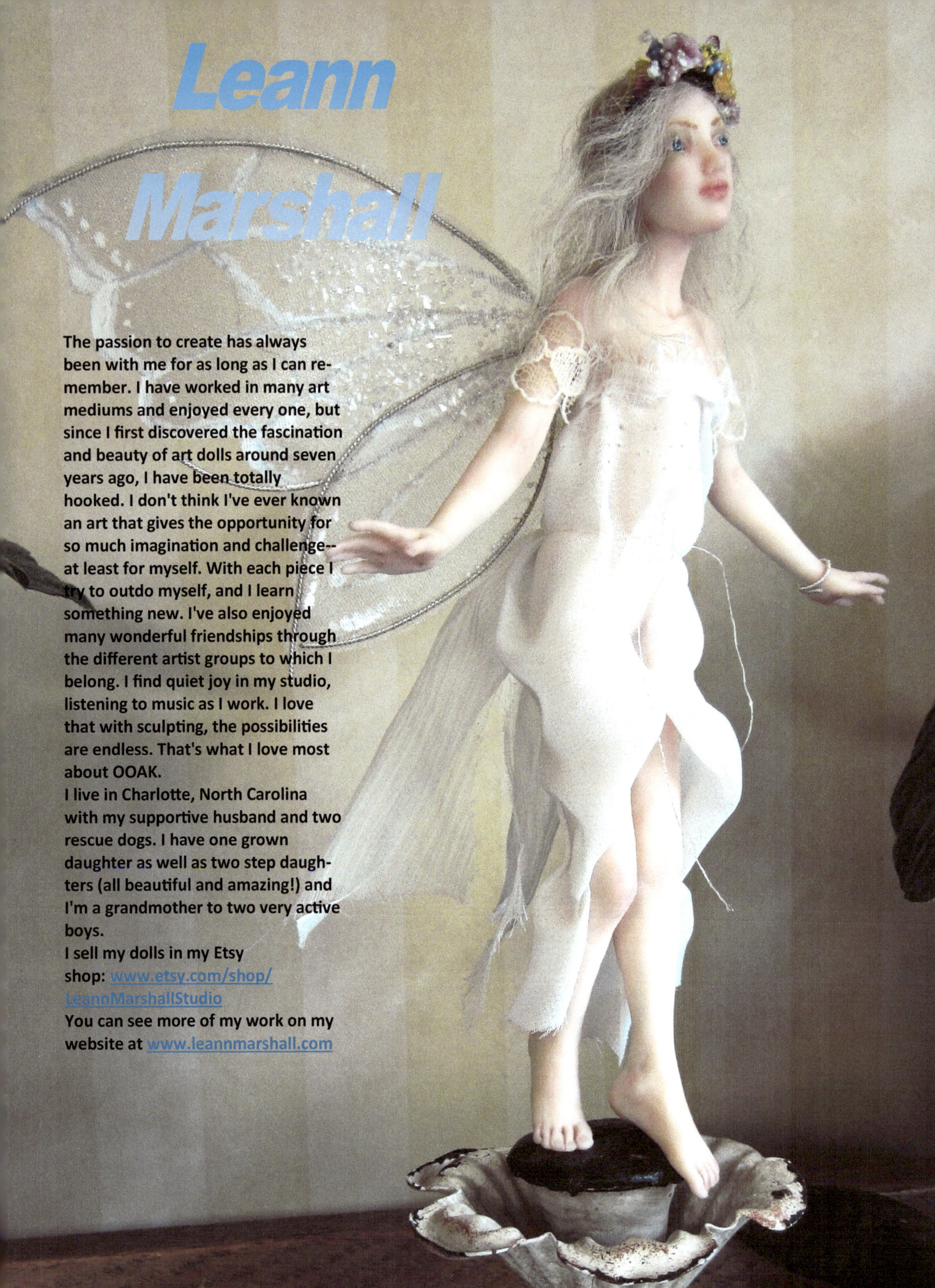

The passion to create has always been with me for as long as I can remember. I have worked in many art mediums and enjoyed every one, but since I first discovered the fascination and beauty of art dolls around seven years ago, I have been totally hooked. I don't think I've ever known an art that gives the opportunity for so much imagination and challenge-- at least for myself. With each piece I try to outdo myself, and I learn something new. I've also enjoyed many wonderful friendships through the different artist groups to which I belong. I find quiet joy in my studio, listening to music as I work. I love that with sculpting, the possibilities are endless. That's what I love most about OOAK.

I live in Charlotte, North Carolina with my supportive husband and two rescue dogs. I have one grown daughter as well as two step daughters (all beautiful and amazing!) and I'm a grandmother to two very active boys.

I sell my dolls in my Etsy shop: www.etsy.com/shop/LeannMarshallStudio

You can see more of my work on my website at www.leannmarshall.com

Hope Mason

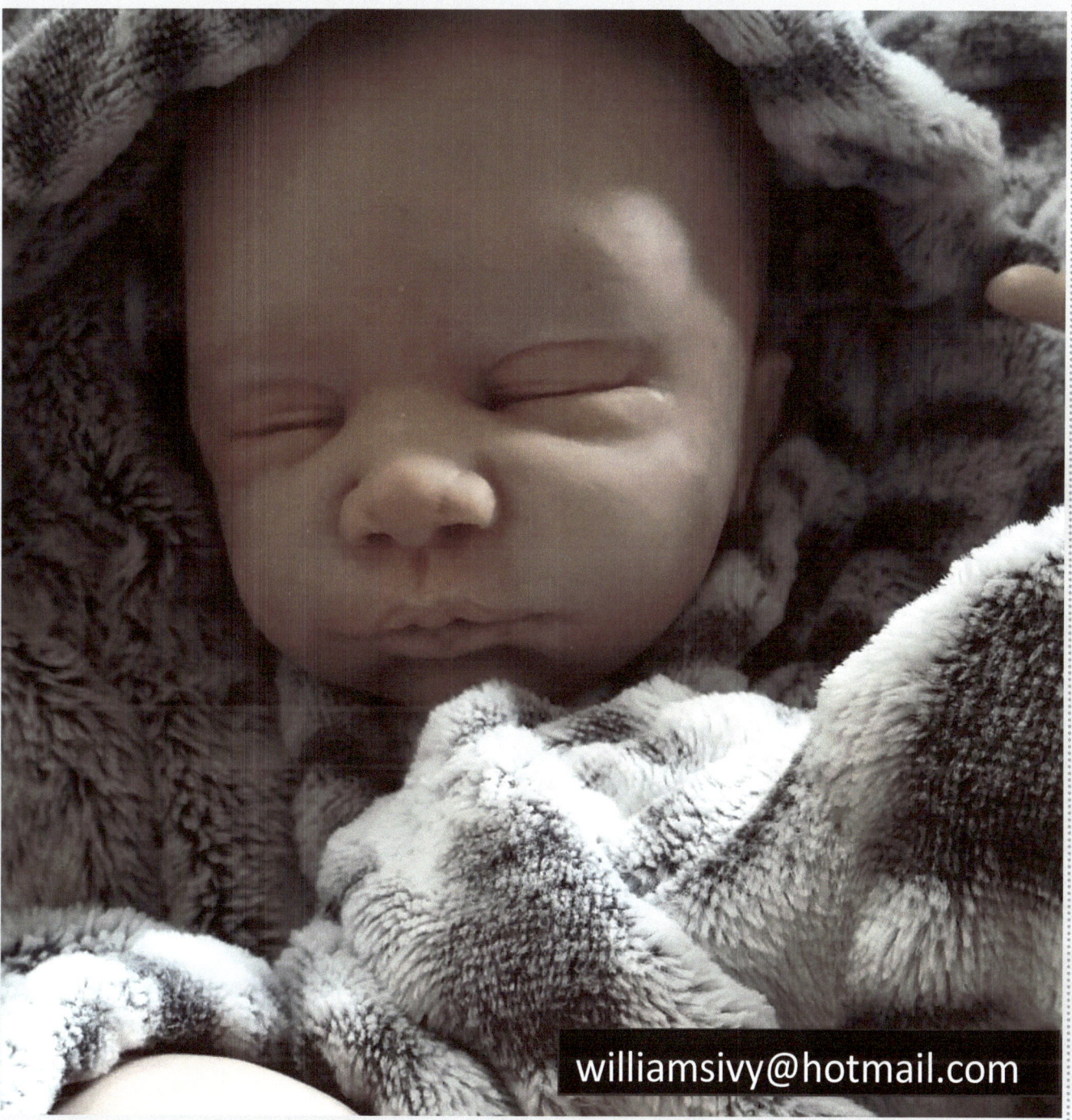

williamsivy@hotmail.com

Working With Worbla

By Cherie Fretto

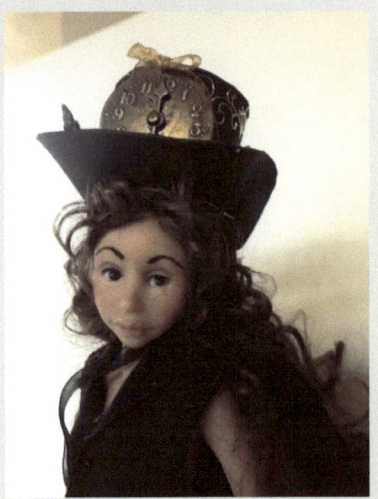

Worbla is a brand of thermoplastic modelling material popular among cosplayers for creating costumes, armor and props. In order to be shaped, Worbla is warmed up, usually with a hot air gun, until it becomes formable. The inbuilt adhesive allows multiple layers or edges to be laminated together. Worbla is available in several colors including clear, white, black and beige. I use Worbla for hats, corsets and boots. It can be easily painted with acrylic paints and decorated with your chosen accessories. I was introduced to Worbla by our wonderful doll artist Gayle Wray.

As I love making top hats, I am showing instructions on making a hat, with several varieties in accessories added to the hat. You will love working with Worbla.

Making a Top Hat

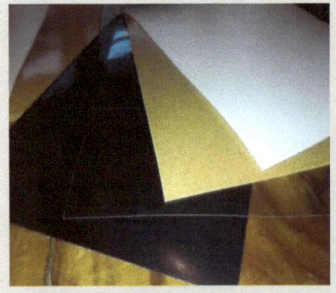 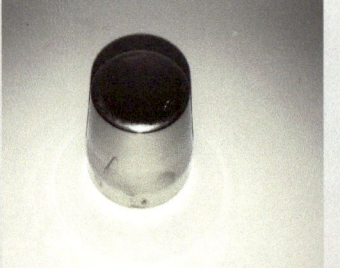 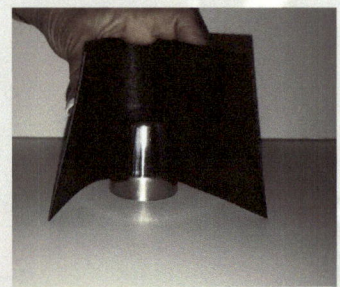 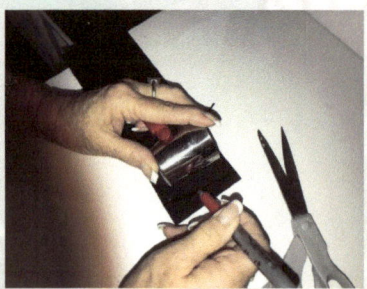

Select the Worbla color you would like to use. Any of the colors can be nicely painted so if you don't have the color of choice you can paint it. In making a Top Hat, I chose a shot glass to use to wrap the Worbla. The shot glass is wider on the top than the bottom so it is the perfect measurement for a Top Hat. If you would like, you can size it so the bottom of the hat is the size of your dolls head. Above I used a magic marker to draw a line to cut as it is an uneven cut with the sizing.

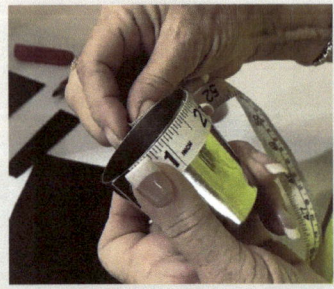 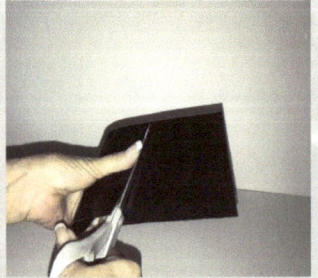 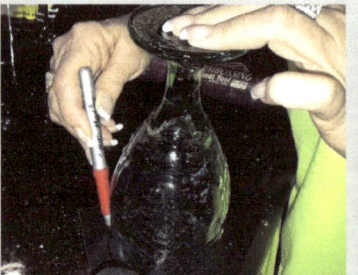 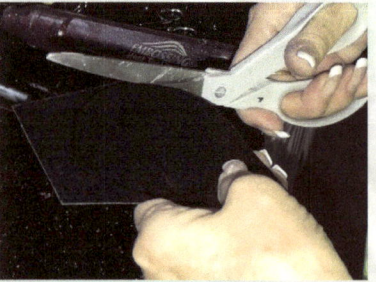

Measure carefully your items for patterns as you don't want to waste any Worbla. You can use things like a glass to draw circles and then cut out. We need the side of the hat, a circle for the top of the hat and a circle for the brim of the hat.

cheriefretto@gmail.com

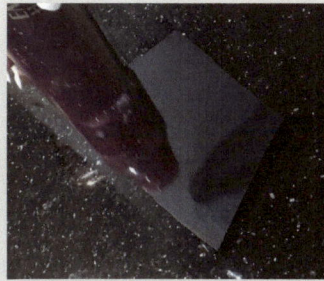 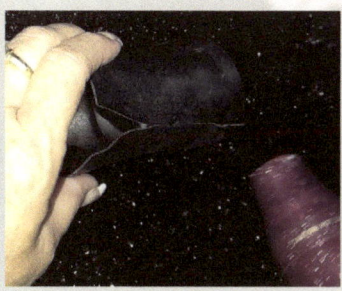 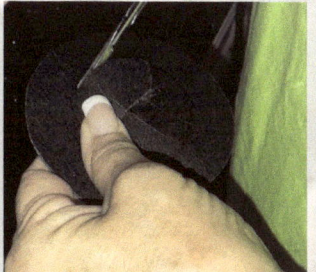 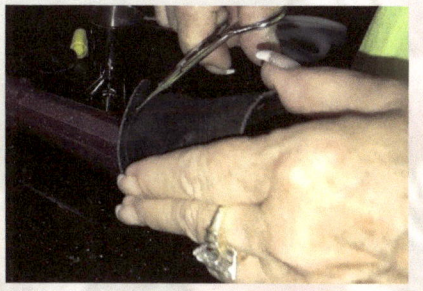

Once you have the size you would like, put the Worbla on a hard surface that will not burn and use a heat gun to soften. This takes practice, as if you get it too hot the Worbla will start to wrinkle. Put your sides together, heat the seam and the sides will stick together. Now cut a circle the exact size of the top of the hat. If it is a little big you can always trim, but you cannot make it larger. Heat the circle and place it on the top of the hat, holding it until it sticks together.

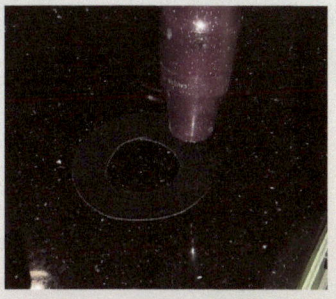 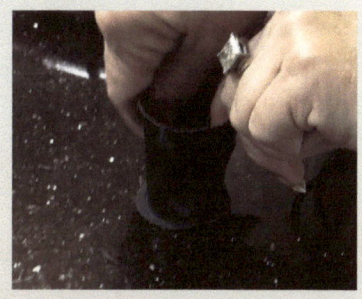 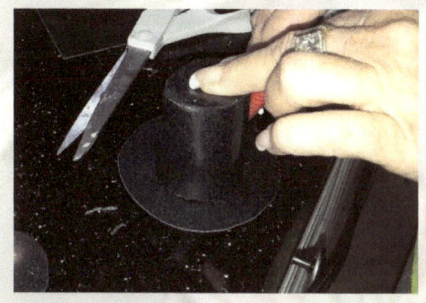

Now cut a circle the exact size of the top of the hat. If it is a little big you can always trim, but you cannot make it larger. Heat the circle and place on the top of the hat, holding it so it sticks together Now cut a circle for the hat brim, making it as large as you would like. Cut out the center of the brim making it slightly smaller than of the bottom of the hat and and remove the circle. Use the same method with the heat gun to attach. You have now completed your Top Hat and have fun decorating with flowers, beads, ribbon or any accessories you like.

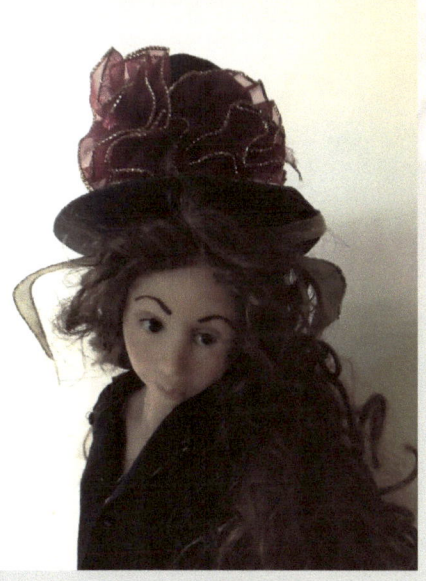

The picture on the left is the hat we just made. The picture on the right was made with Worbla as a base and coated with thick paint and sparkle beads.

There are many uses for Worbla including corsets, boots, shoes, arm bands, pocketbooks or any item you want to look like simulated leather.

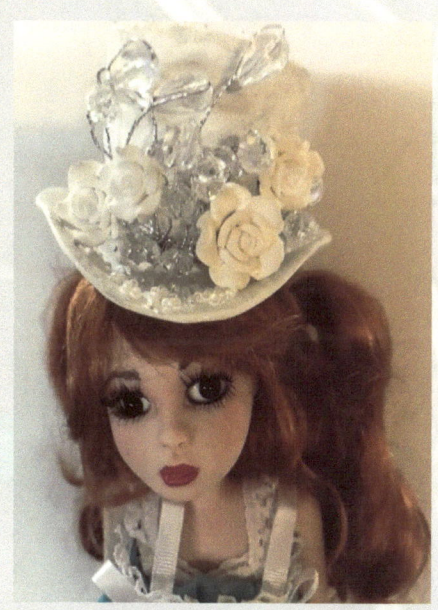

Griselda's Dancing Shoes

By Leslie Duthie

A Needle felting Tutorial by MisPlace Dolls
misplacedolls@hotmail.com

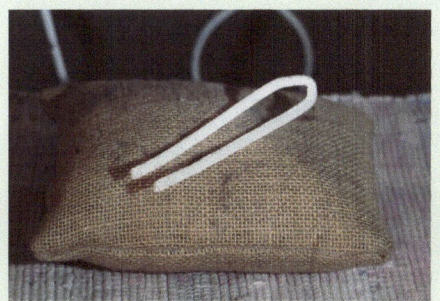

Start with a 12 1/4 inch long chenille pipe cleaner—fold in half.

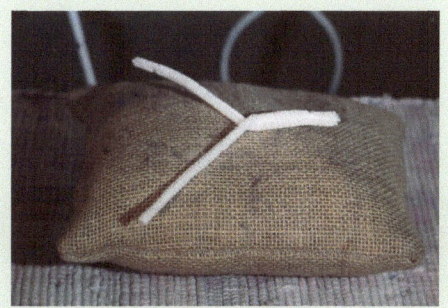

Twist the pipe cleaner (from the folded end) down a couple of inches. How long this twisted length needs to be depends on how much the toes are to curl.

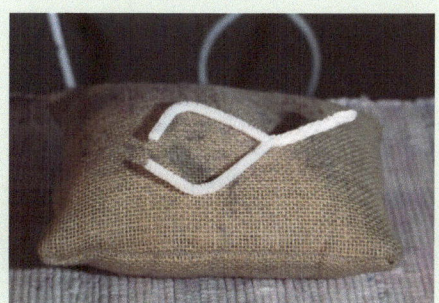

Take the ends of the pipe cleaner and bend them back towards each other. This is the framework for the base of the shoe. This width and length should reflect the size of the shoe for the character's foot.

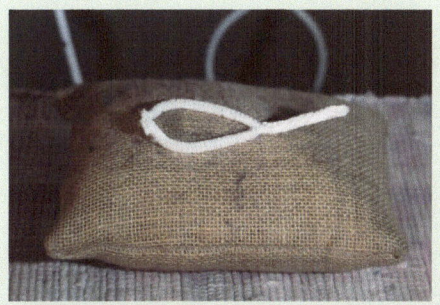

Taking the ends of the pipe cleaner, twist them together to complete the loop.

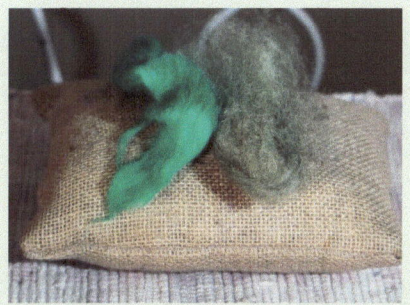

Choose your color choices. One color is good, two are better. Lay one color on top of the other.

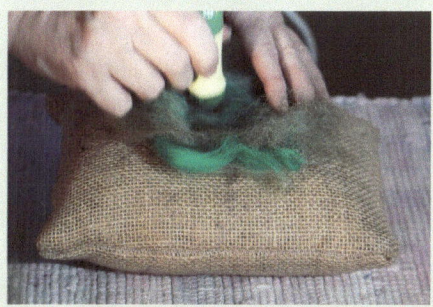

Then taking my multiple needle felter tool – pushing it in and out of the roving wool, I create a flat piece of "material".

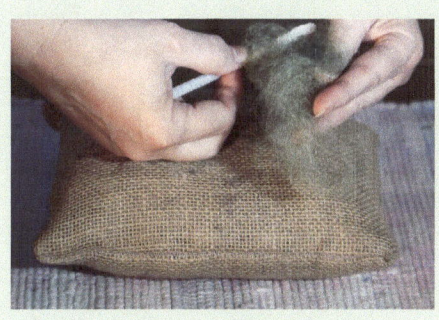

After finishing my "material", I take another piece of roving wool and wrap it around the end of the pipe cleaner shoe that I had twisted together to make the curl of the toes.

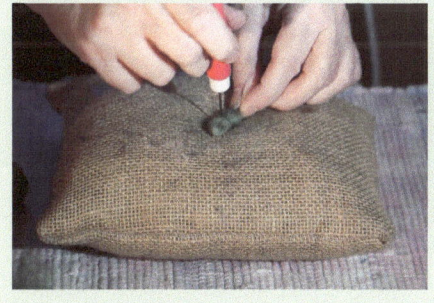

After wrapping it around the end of the pipe cleaner, I take my single felting needle and secure the wool in place with a few pokes of the needle.

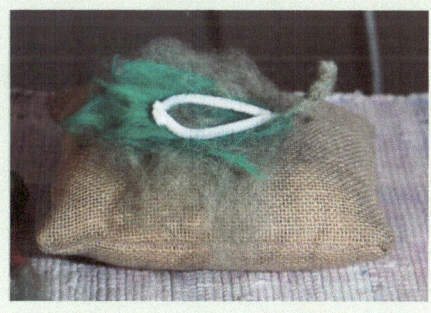

Now I take the "material" that I had created earlier and place it under the pipe cleaner frame. I then pull that up and around the pipe cleaner.

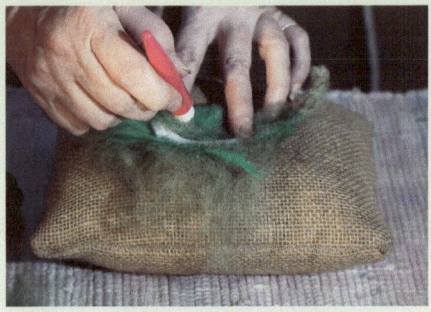
I then take my single felting needle and start securing the felt around the frame by poking the wool with my needle.

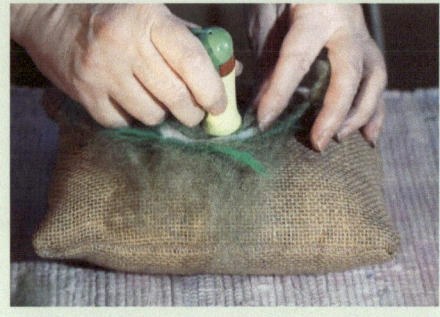
For the larger flat areas, I use my multiple needle tool and continue to wrap the felt around the frame.

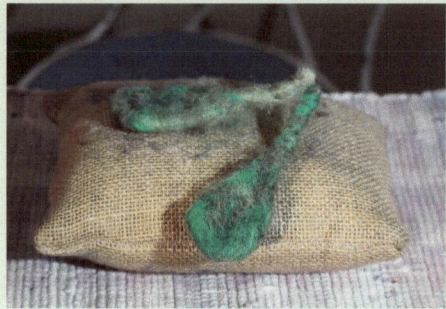
When I am done working the wool, I have two flat pieces to be used for the base of the shoes.

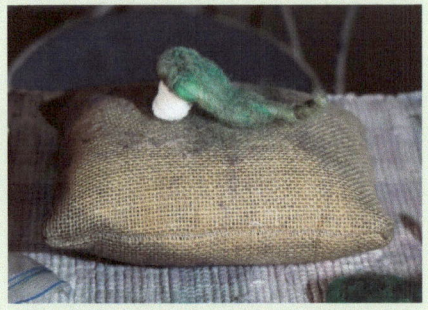
I decided I was going to have a little fun with this project and added a heel. This is more like a slipper shoe for Griselda. I take one piece of pipe cleaner and wrap it around my finger like a cork screw. I then wrapped roving wool around the heel.

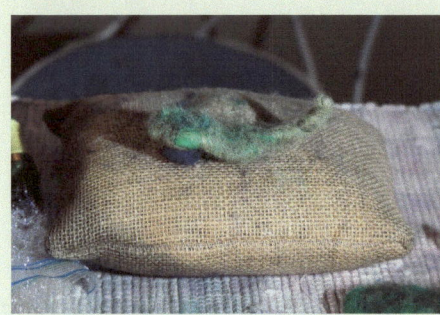
After wrapping the wool around the heel, I attached it to the base of the shoe with a little more wool. I also put a bend in the shoe like what a high heel shoe would have.

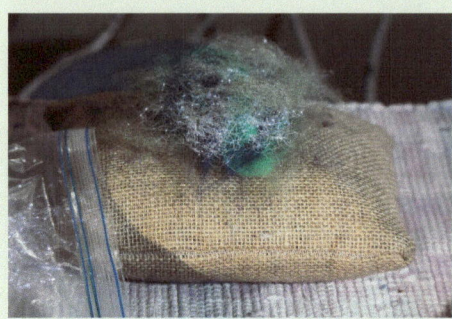
Now I needed to make the top of the shoe. I wanted a little bling, so I added a little blue roving wool and some Angelina's spark to my layering process.

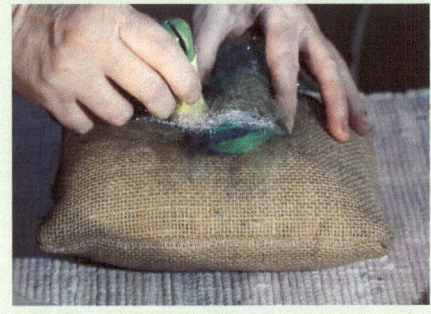
This piece requires felting in a triangle shape more than just a flat piece. Once I have my triangle felted, I lay it across the front of the shoe to see if I have it large enough.

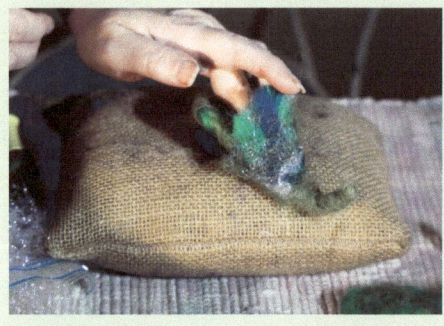
I then secure the side of the triangle to the side of the shoe with some more needle felting.

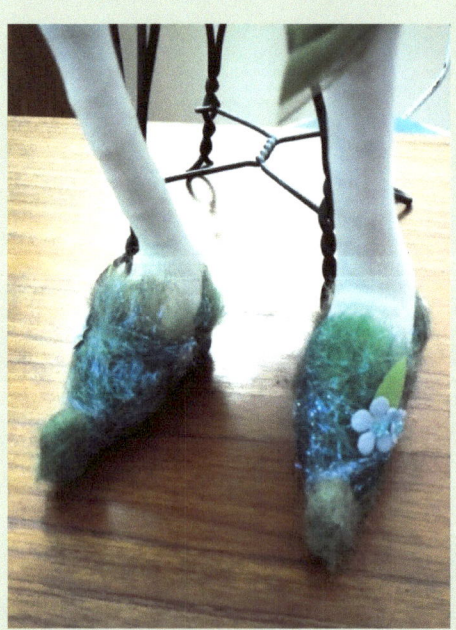

Finally, I add some flowers and some beads to the top of my shoes and curled the ends of the pipe cleaners back for the whimsical look of a magical shoe.

Hope you have enjoyed this tutorial. The original idea for the shoes came from Sarafina's Fiber Arts youtube.com with tweaks of my own. Incidentally, Griselda loves her new dancing shoes.

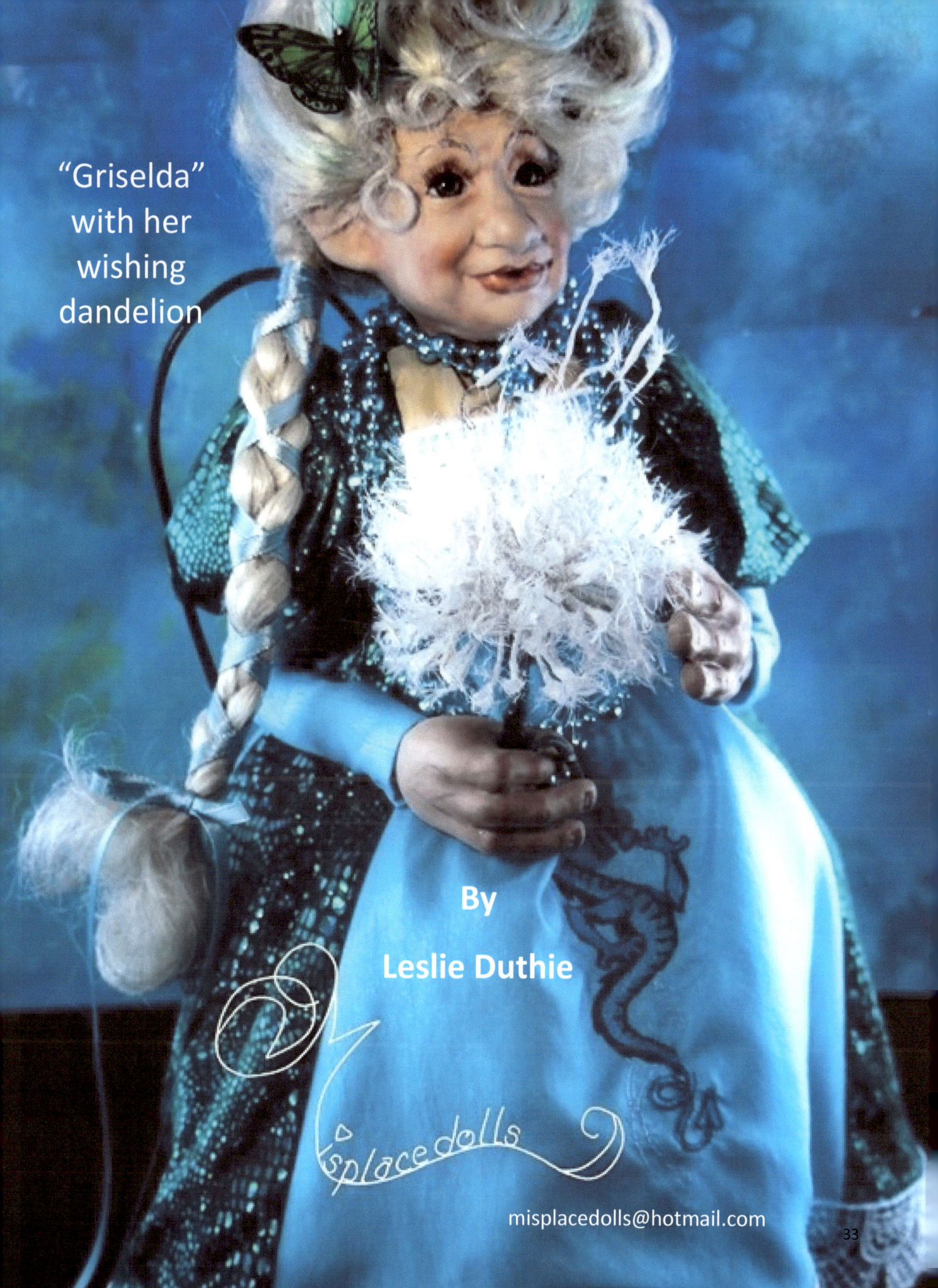

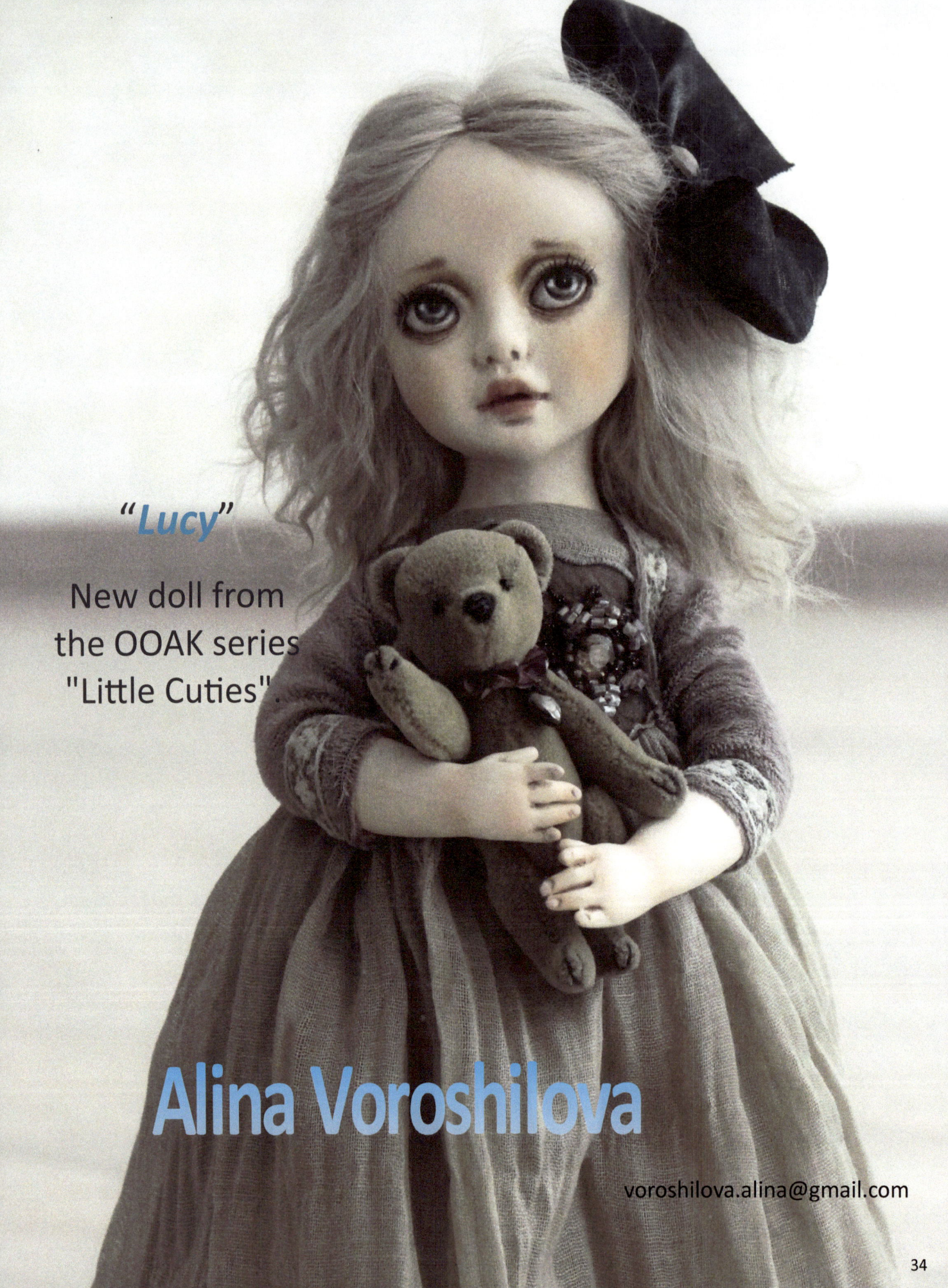

"Lucy"

New doll from the OOAK series "Little Cuties".

Alina Voroshilova

voroshilova.alina@gmail.com

Accessories: Love Them or Hate Them

Dennis R. Slate

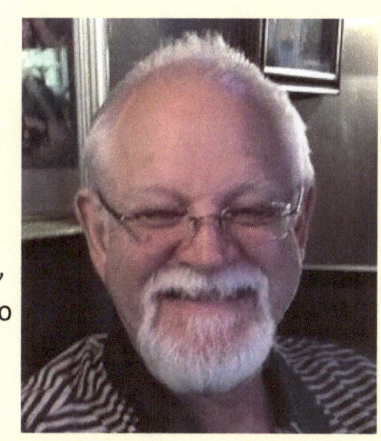

I have always enjoyed making and sculpting dolls. Adding accessories to your doll is always a plus. Your artistic work needs to tell a story of what you have created. For example: An old man dressed in a Santa Claus outfit may look like Santa Claus but, adding a bag stuffed full of toys and him holding a toy in his hand leaves no doubt who the doll is. The addition of the toys to the doll gives clarification to the potential customer and helps the customer to warm up to your doll.

Accessories can be made or purchased. Rarely does the artist find the exact size or piece they wish to use with the doll. The material for any accessory can be made out of paper or polymer clay, wood, fabric or metal. What you choose for your material will be determined by weight, originality, and your ability to make the item. If you wish to make a Teddy Bear, fabric would be my choice. Using needle and thread (or sewing machine) this item can be made. Additionally, you could use Fabritac glue instead of sewing the accessory. This would be lightweight and correct for the doll. Paper clay is extremely light and very forgiving when shaping your item, and it can be easily painted. Polymer clay is what most doll makers use but not all therefore, the only comment to make is the weight of polymer clay is sometimes too heavy. Wood is another material that a lot of dollmakers use. Balsam wood is extremely lightweight and easily carved with a Dremel tool. I have yet to use metal, but my choice would be aluminum. These are just a few choices in material, but the sky is the limit!

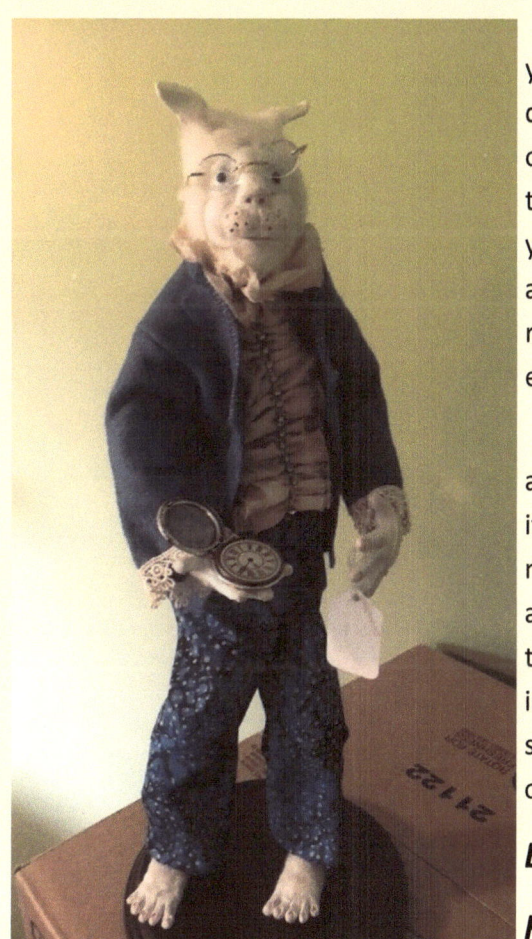

Another approach is to be always be on the lookout for items you might use to enhance your work. Sometimes your inspiration for the doll will come from an accessory. Finding the correct size, weight, color or the effect needed for your accessory is almost never found, leaving the dollmaker to make their own. Always be on the lookout everywhere you go for accessories. Some of the places where I have had the best luck are Hobby Lobby, Michaels, other local craft stores and even Cracker Barrel. Other places we have had some success are flea markets, yard sales, estate sales and even antique shows.

When someone is purchasing a doll where you did not make the accessories you should let the purchaser know. It could have been the item was the reason the doll was created. Also, on the same note if you made them let them know that. Never copy someone's work unless you ask them if it is ok and if it is you must give them credit for the design of the accessory. Every dollmaker decorates their items differently. In ending this short discussion, if you cannot get the effect you want then you should make your own accessories. Remember to always color co-ordinate and detail your item to get the effect you were looking for.

Email: dslate@northstate.net

Facebook: Seasons-Past@SeasonsPastdolls

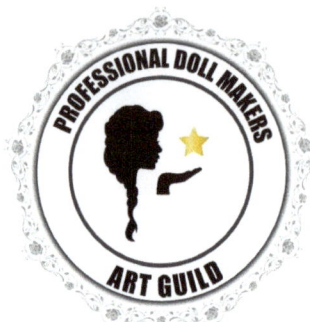

Learning To Sculpt

Professional Doll Makers Art Guild Mentor-Apprentice Program

Thoughts from:

Sherry Woolsey Neilson

My name is Sherrie Neilson and I am currently an apprentice in the PDMAG Intermediate Academy. I have recently completed the last challenge where the apprentice's were given three photos to choose from. The photos to choose from consisted of two girls and a rooster, I choe the rooster thinking I wanted to go out side of my comfort zone of making fairies and character dolls. My rooster was defiantly a challenge and more then once I wished I had chosen one of the other photos, I think anything that could go wrong with a sculpt went wrong with my sculpt, I was starting to think my sculpt was cursed. I started out sculpting each and every one of the feathers by hand, by the time I had finished the two legs I was exhausted and realized it was taking to much time and I would never have the rooster completed by the deadline, so I decided to make molds of my feathers to speed up the process. I ran into several issues with the rooster such as several brakes after falling from my table and standing issues that had me frustrated and ready to through in the towel, but with the support of my mentor and fellow apprentices I pushed through to the end. I am so proud of my finished piece not just for the awe of WOW I did that, but from the challenges I over came and learned from. If you are looking for an amazing group to start sculpting or to just perfect your skill in doll making, I would defiantly suggest the PDMAG Intermediate Academy. The mentors and apprentices are all amazing and so supportive with their gentle advice and of course my favorite, the challenges that keeps you busy and perfecting your skill's.

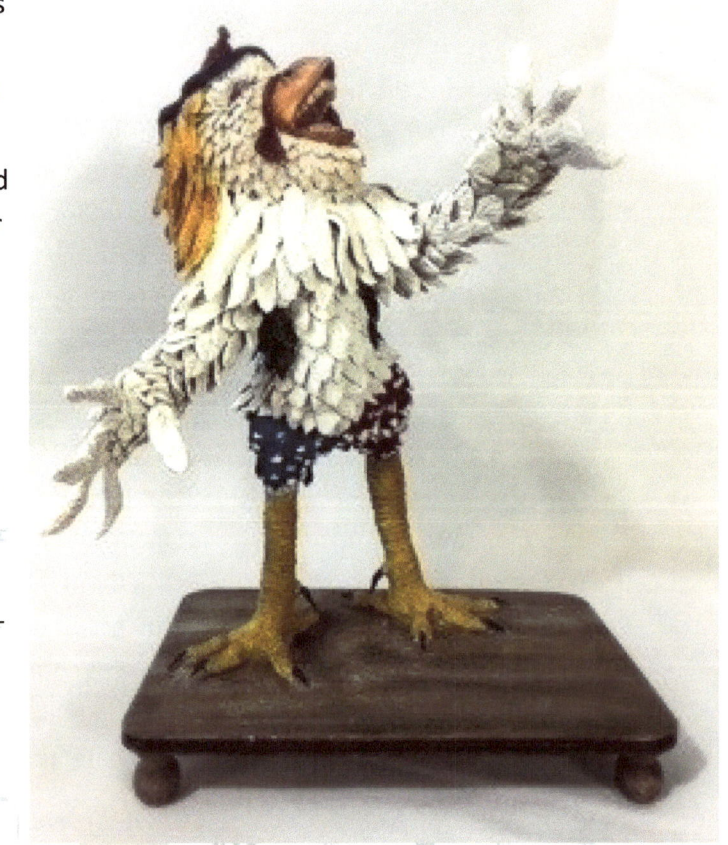

The Professional Doll Makers Apprentice Program

Our program is all about learning what makes an OOAK really special. We work on wigging, costuming, adding movement, gesture and life into our Apprentice's work. The Apprentice's are already well on their way to being a great sculptors and our Master Artist group is here to help them turn their hard work into a successful career in doll making.

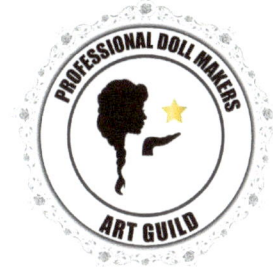

Thoughts from:

Cecelia Arrington

I was initially intimidated by the challenge, but once I took a good look at her face, I just couldn't resist duplicating her! I used 24 gage wire to make her frame. Then I used aluminum foil to shape her torso & neck and then I used masking tape to cover the foil. I prefer thin limbs, so I used masking tape to shape the legs and arms.

She is made Premiere air dry clay that was tinted with orange paint to give her a flesh tone. Her eyes are acrylic. Her cheeks, eyes and forehead are colored from pastels and I used paint for her lips.

Her clothes are made from scraps from G Street Fabrics in Rockville MD. My philosophy is to reuse/repurpose whatever I can find for clothing. I rarely buy new fabrics. All of my dolls clothing comes from the Goodwill or the scraps at fabric stores.

Her hair is made from yarn glued to a wig cap. I always buy thick single strand yarn because it resembles hair already and doesn't need much combing or straightening. I combed the yarn, then flat ironed it. Her wig cap is made of pale burlap I purchased from Joanne's.

My tools of choice for sculpting are toothpicks, sewing needles and wax carvers. I used wet dry sandpaper to smooth her.

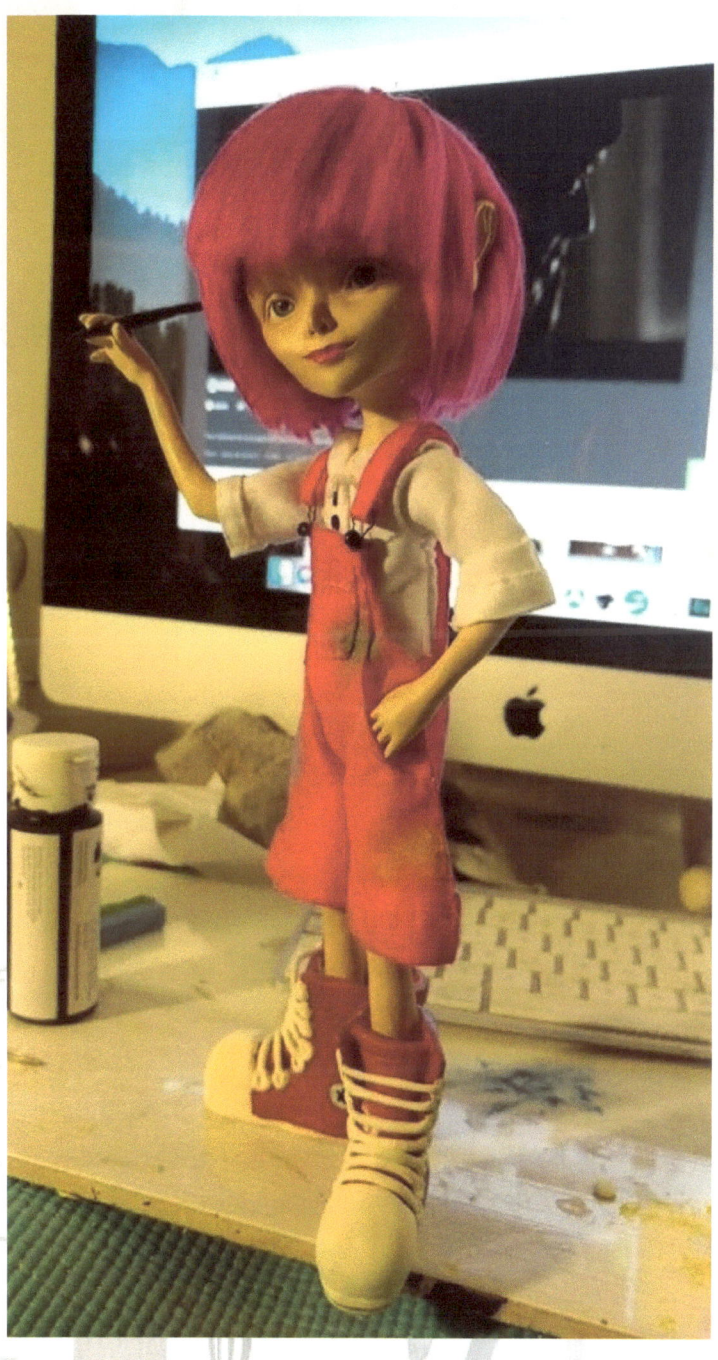

Thoughts from:
Aleksandra Wright

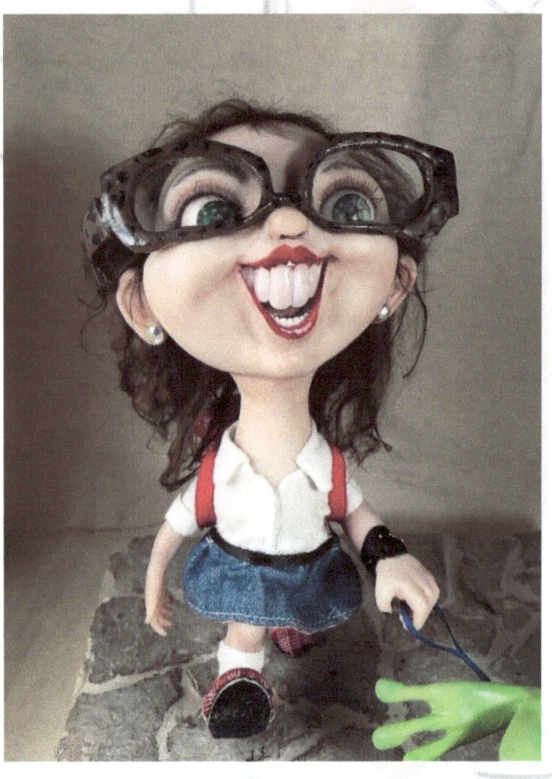

This has been a fun challenge of converting an image into a 3D sculpture. It's an excellent way of learning depth perception and perspective. It made me step out of my comfort zone and try my hand at a caricature. This challenge also provided me with a venue of trying out something different, something that I normally would not have tried on my own. It was invaluable experience

The Academy teaches:

Sculpting

Accessories

Wigging

Teeth

Outfitting

Just Being Creative

Thoughts from:
Pam Titensor

I had so much fun doing the recent challenge. It was fun and yet challenging, I've never tried any kind of animal or creature before. The open mouth and teeth were also new to me. That's what I love about doing the challenges, they take me out of my comfort zone! I have learned so much sense joining the Professional Doll Makers Art Guild. ! I love it so much and have learned so much! The mentor program is wonderful, knowing you have someone to turn to for help, and cheer you on. Thank you for all your hard work!

Join us at:

Professionaldollmakers.com

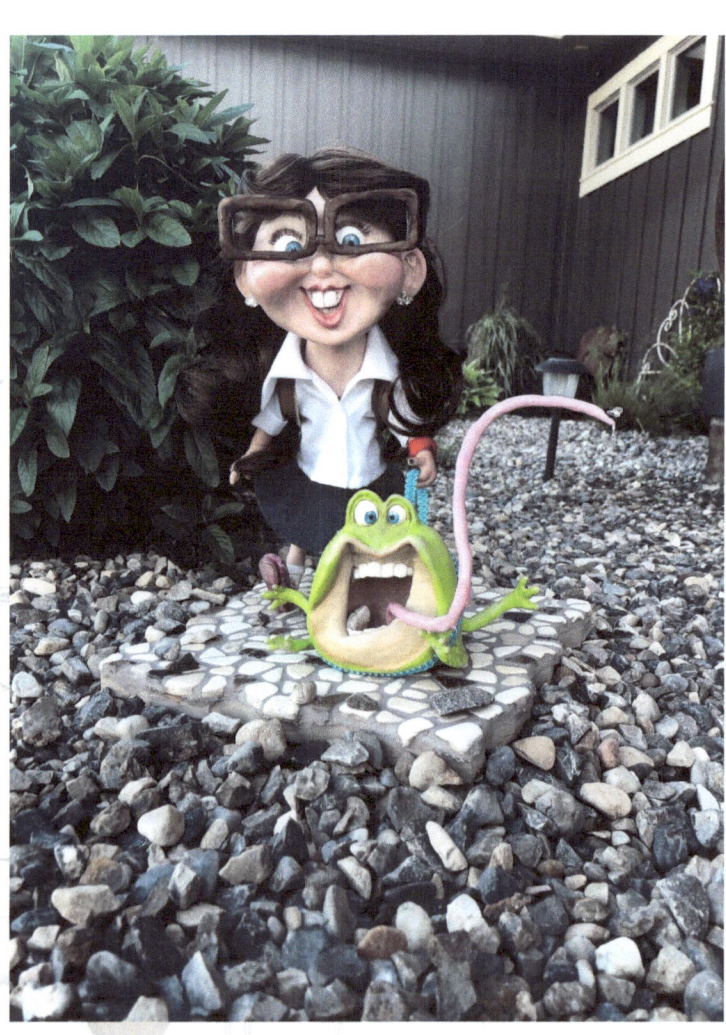

Vihareva Pechenkina

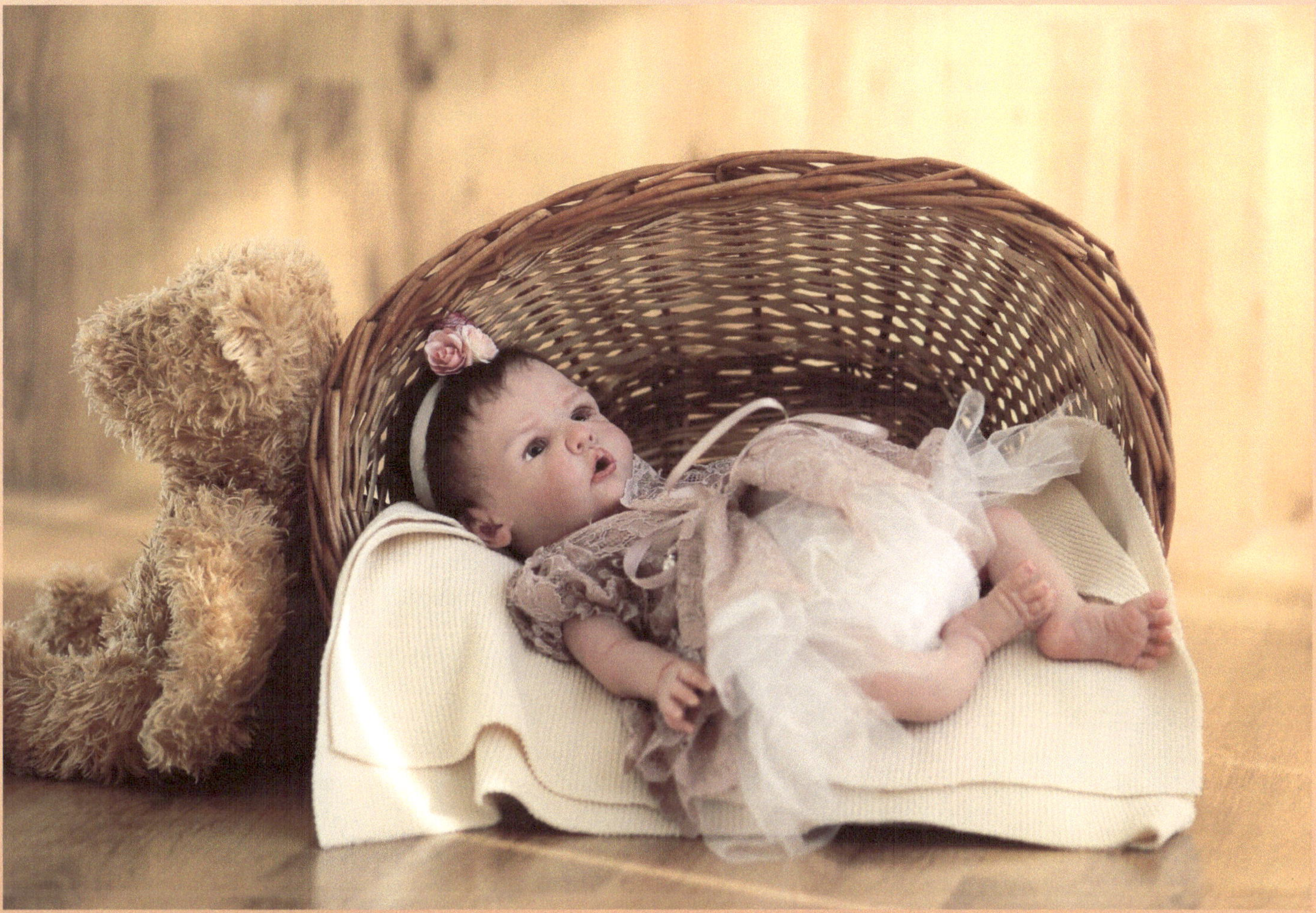

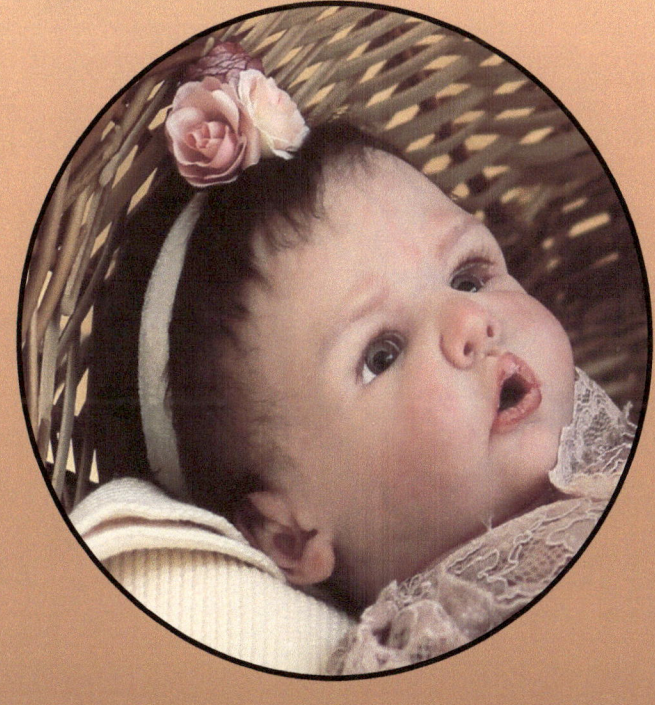

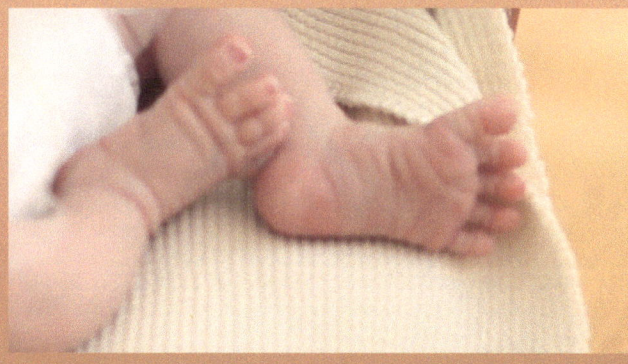

victoria-vihareva@rambler.ru

Casting Your Own Doll Accessories

by Maria Grover

I enjoy creating all sizes of silicone baby dolls! Having spent several years as a newborn photographer, I love being able to recreate all the fine details of a precious new life. And while working on life size babies gives me the opportunity to really make a baby doll true to life, I've come to also enjoy creating miniature babies. Over the past few years I've found that many collectors love tiny lifelike babies, and the little ones are so fun to create! However, when sculpting and producing miniature babies, it is not as easy to find outfits and accessories for them as it is for life size babies. Naturally with a life size baby, you can purchase real baby clothing, pacifiers, bottles, bracelets, and so on. But with little miniature babies, many of the accessories are made by hand. Accessories such as pacifiers and rattles are often sculpted from polymer clay, and thus aren't as durable since it is easy for little parts to break off when being used with the doll. It is also very tedious to sculpt a new set of accessories for each doll when producing an edition of a sculpt. So I started casting some of my accessories, such as miniature pacifiers, in resin.

For those who have never tried casting something before, I thought it might be helpful to share a very basic beginner's guide to molding and casting. In this example, I will be recreating little pacifiers. However, you can use this beginner's guide to make castings of any accessories that have a flat side to them. The materials I used to mold and cast come from Smooth-On.com, although I have also seen them on Amazon and equivalent supplies in various art shops.

First I begin by using polymer clay to sculpt itty bitty pacifiers that will fit the mouths of my dolls. Once the pacifiers are baked and cooled, I place each finished pacifier into a small disposable container. In this instance, I use a medicine measuring cup and put a tiny dab of glue on the bottom of the pacifier to hold it in place inside the measuring cup. Once the pacifier is securely in place it is time for the silicone!

I chose to use EcoFlex 30 for this particular mold because, since the object I am casting is so tiny, I needed a silicone that was more viscous and could easily get around the tiny parts without creating a lot of air pockets. I also wanted my mold to be flexible enough for me to easily manipulate the sides to help get air bubbles out while still being firm enough to hold its shape well. Dragon Skin, Oomoo, and others will also work, depending on the size and shape of your mold. Each line of silicone has varying viscosities and generally speaking, the higher the number, the firmer it will be once cured.

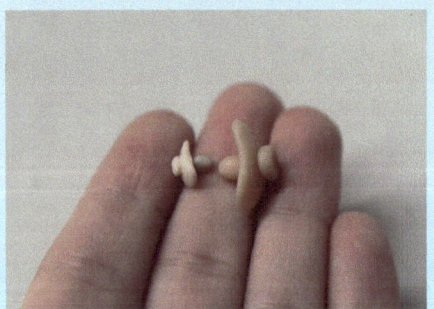
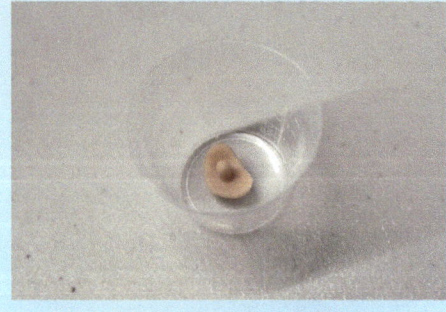
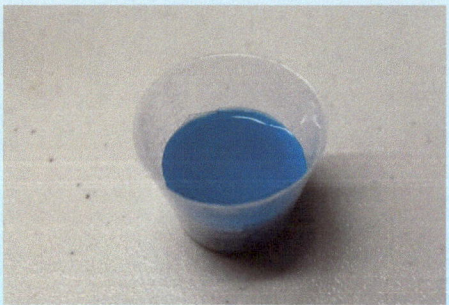
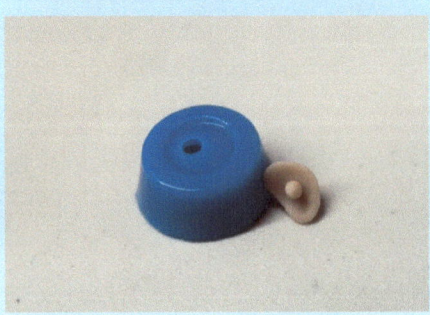
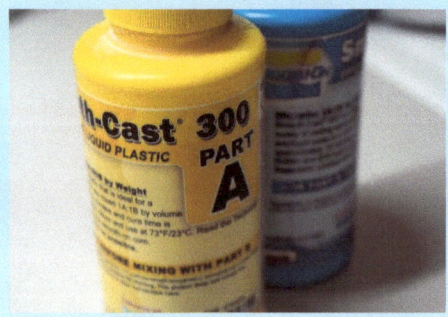
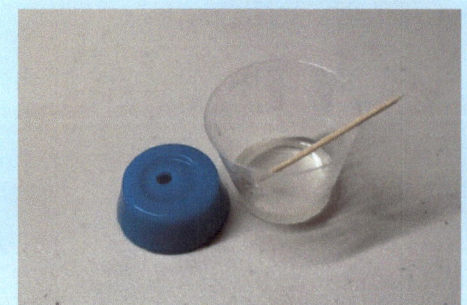

Different silicones also have different lengths of time for working and varying cure times, so be sure to check out the technical bulletins for each product to make sure it will fit your needs.

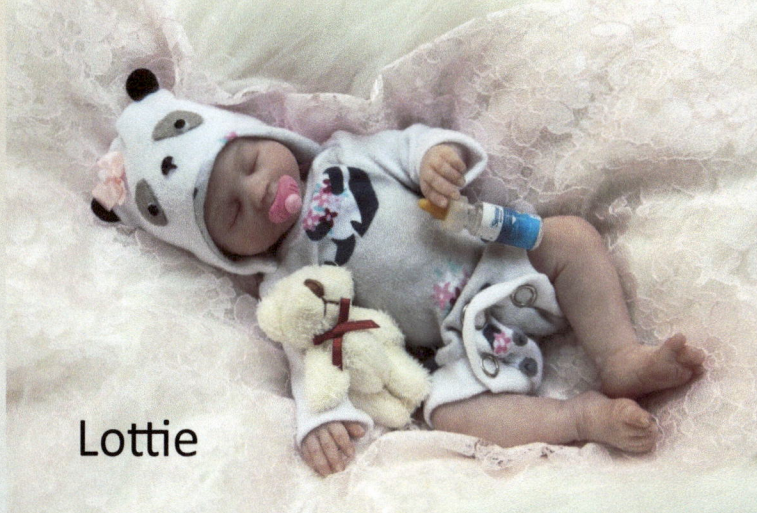

Lottie

When mixing the EcoFlex 30, the ratio needs to be 1:1 of Part A to Part B. The pot life for EcoFlex 30 is technically 45 minutes, though I have found that it is best to keep your working time to around 20 minutes or less when working with small quantities like in this example. (The silicone is clear by default, though I have chosen to pigment my silicone blue for this example to make it easier to see in pictures.) Mix together equal parts of A and B, and once thoroughly mixed, you can tap your container on the table to pull air bubbles to the top. Slowly pour the silicone into the container that has your sculpted accessory in it. It is best to pour into the side of the container and allow it to surround your accessory from the bottom up, rather than pouring over the top of the object and potentially creating an air pocket. Once your accessory is completely covered, allow the silicone to fully cure (for EcoFlex 30, this is four hours).

Once cured, you can remove your silicone mold from its container. (To make it easier to remove, I just cut my medicine cup away.) Remove your original sculpted accessory from the mold, and now you are ready to make castings! As with silicone, there are many different types of resin. For these pacifiers, I opted to use Smooth-Cast 300 which cures quickly at only 10 minutes per cast into a firm white resin. Like with the silicone, you will need to mix an equal amount of Part A and Part B. You can choose to pigment your resin before mixing the two parts together or leave it clear and allow it to cure white. Smooth-Cast 300 has only a 3 minute pot life, so you will need to work quickly. Carefully pour the liquid resin into the mold. With these tiny pacifiers, I pour a few drops down into the nipple part of the pacifier, then use a toothpick to shove out any air bubbles, then pour in a bit more and use my toothpick to move the sides of the mold around to help guide the resin into the edges of the main part of the pacifier, and repeat until the mold is full and I'm fairly confident I have filled any air pockets. The resin will start to turn white from the center outward as it cures, and in ten minutes it will be solid white and firm. Once cured you can remove your casting from the mold and paint as desired. And now that you have a mold, you can continue to make many more of your doll's accessories!

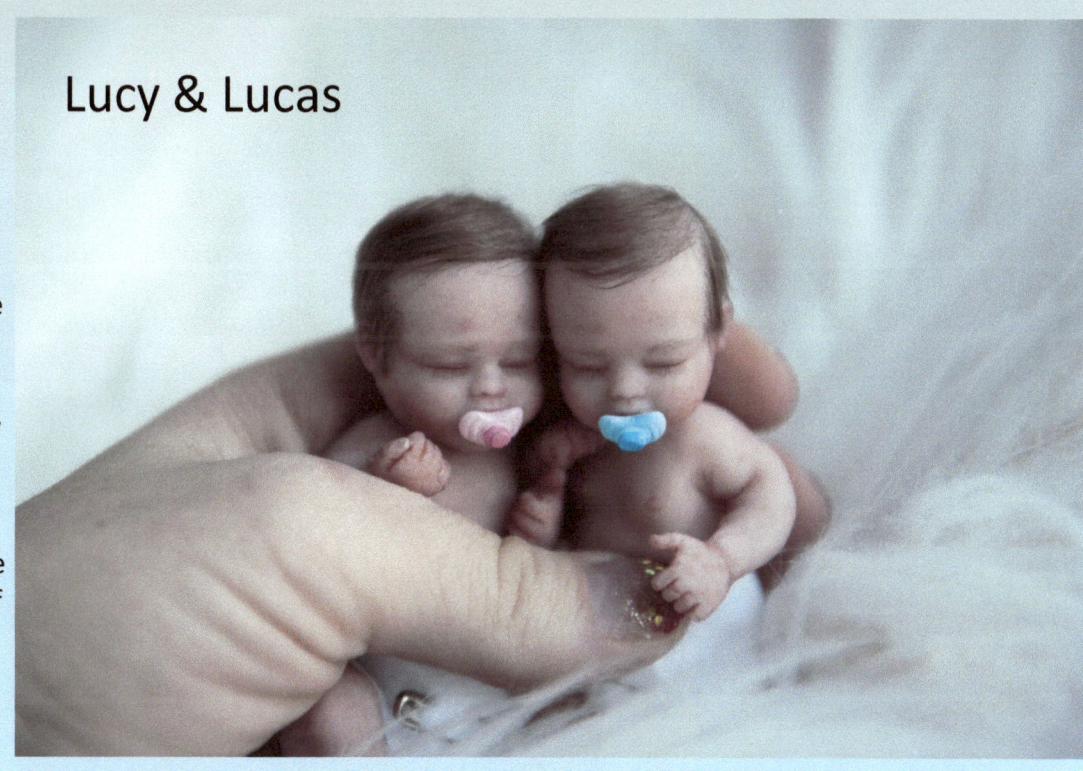

Lucy & Lucas

marialynndolls@gmail.com

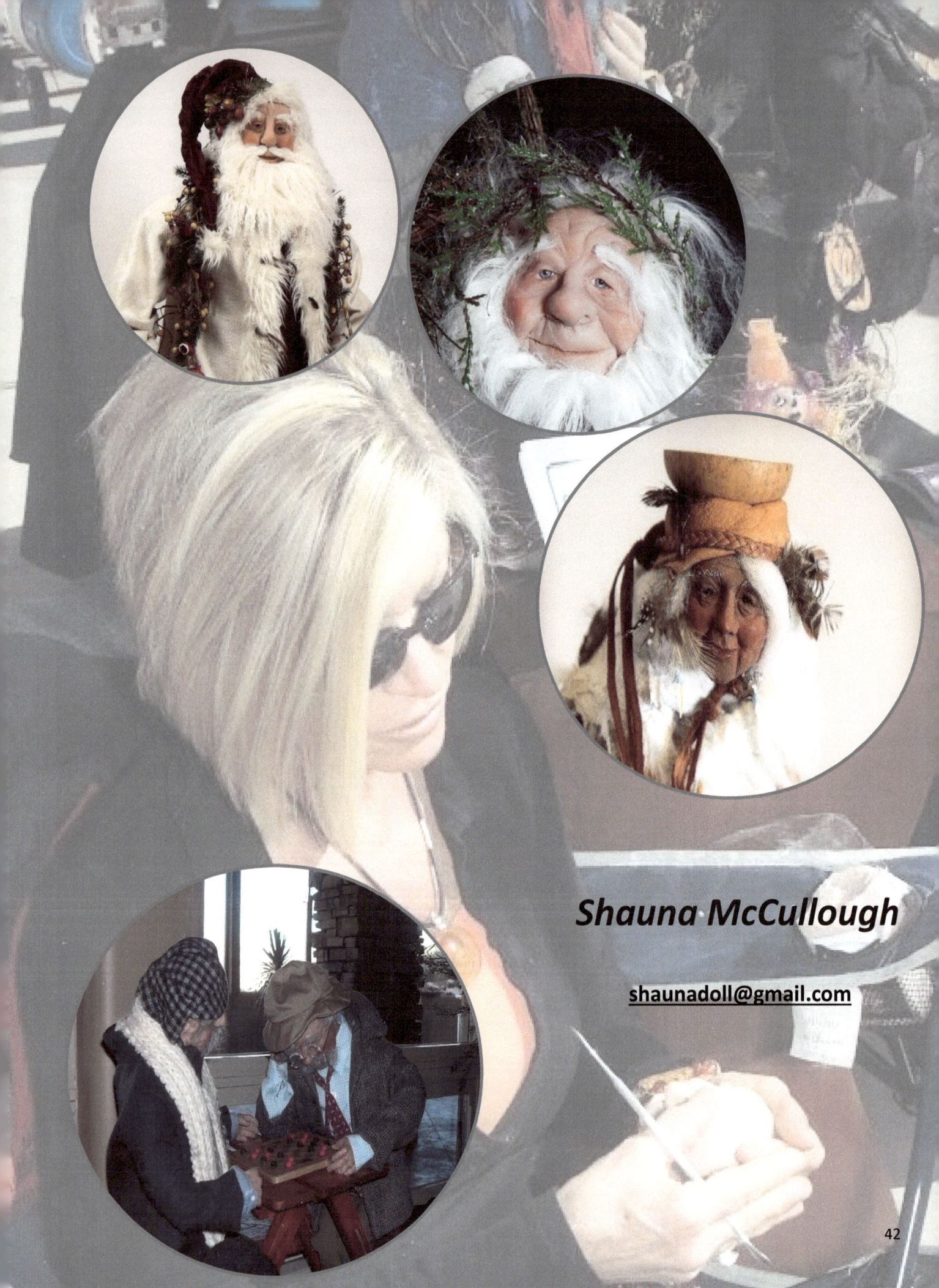

Shauna McCullough

shaunadoll@gmail.com

THE LAND OF MAKE BELIEVE

By Shauna McCullough

Twenty-eight years ago, I became interested in the art of making dolls. The journey that led and inspired me to make one-of-a-kind dolls was rather interesting. My family owned a clothing store in Salt Lake City, Utah. I was in charge of window displays and thought it would be fun to incorporate a Santa or two at Christmas time to kind of spruce things up. I found some bland store bought Santa but I did not care for the look they gave my windows; the funny little dolls did not look quite right in such an elegant holiday window.

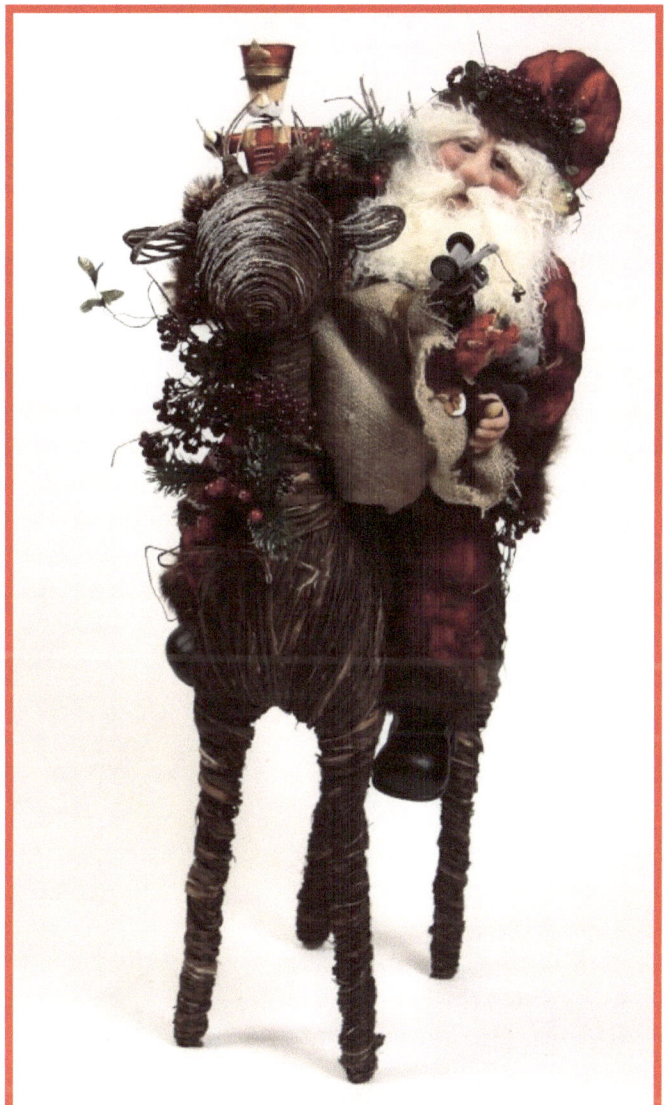

I decided to try my hand at making Santa dolls myself. It was frustrating. I couldn't figure out how to make the heads to stay on and how to have them not tip over. I didn't know what kind of clay to use, so I went to art supply store and bought some clay to make heads and hands for the dolls. I spent hours and hours on one doll. I thought you were suppose to bake this clay in the oven, but to my disappointment, I opened the oven door and found a pile of clay sitting on the cookie sheet (literally a pile of clay).

During the same holiday season, our local newspaper ran an article about a gentleman who was making the kind of dolls I wanted to make. The dolls were all hand-sculpted with a special clay and all had beautiful handmade clothing and were on display at a furniture store of all places. My mom and I immediately went there. What I saw there, changed my life.

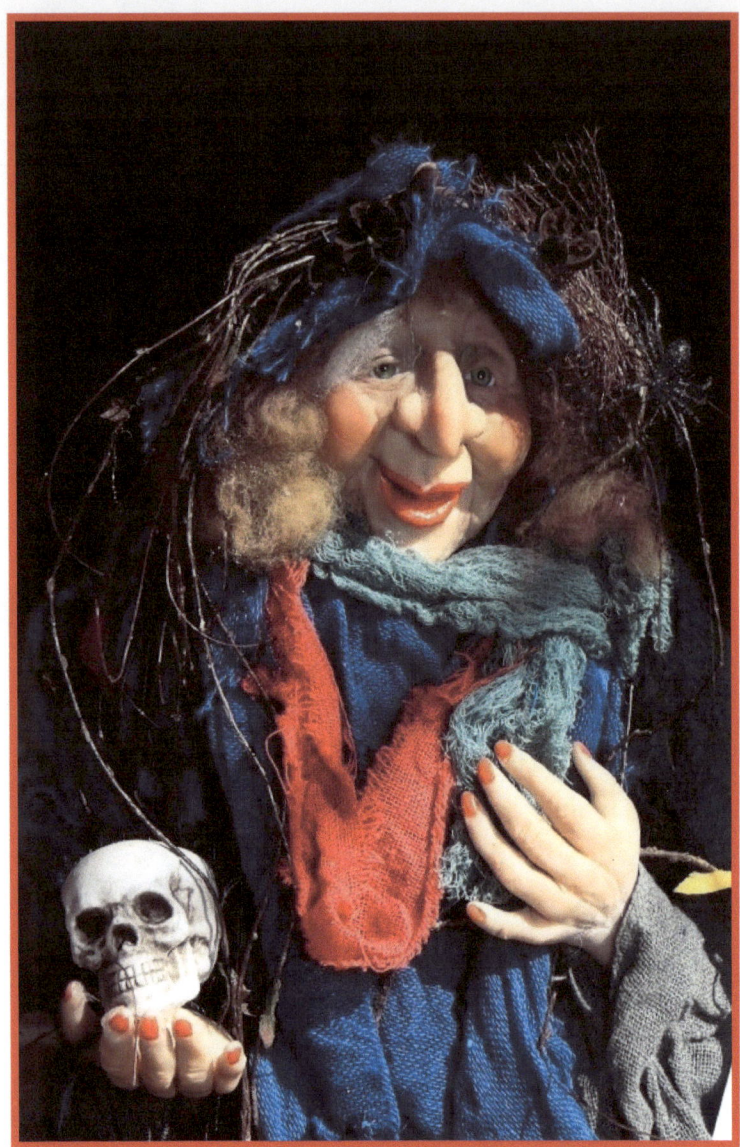

The dolls I saw were the work of a renowned master doll maker.

My mother noticed classes were being offered so she bought one for me as a Christmas gift. My mother is now close to 97 years old and still loves the dolls I learned to make and says it was the best gift she has ever given! She is still my inspiration and continues to support my love for doll making.

My window display became a form of art and as people would pass by they would stop and admire the art dolls and inquire if the dolls were for sale. Every evening after work, I would go home and work on new creations and all my dolls would sell. I am sure I spent more time and money on them than I actually made on them, but it didn't matter because my customers loved my dolls almost as much as I loved making them!

Fast forward 28 years, my custom studio is a landscape of heads, hands, and feet with boxes of plush wonderful textiles and accessories to fit any doll. I love making Santa but my desire to expand has opened a new world of many kinds of Art Dolls from Native American, African and of course my 'make-believe' Ethereal dolls.

Once the doll is complete they take on a life of their own and hopefully be a feast for the eyes and of the heart. I love the art of making dolls and may the journey continue for many years to come.

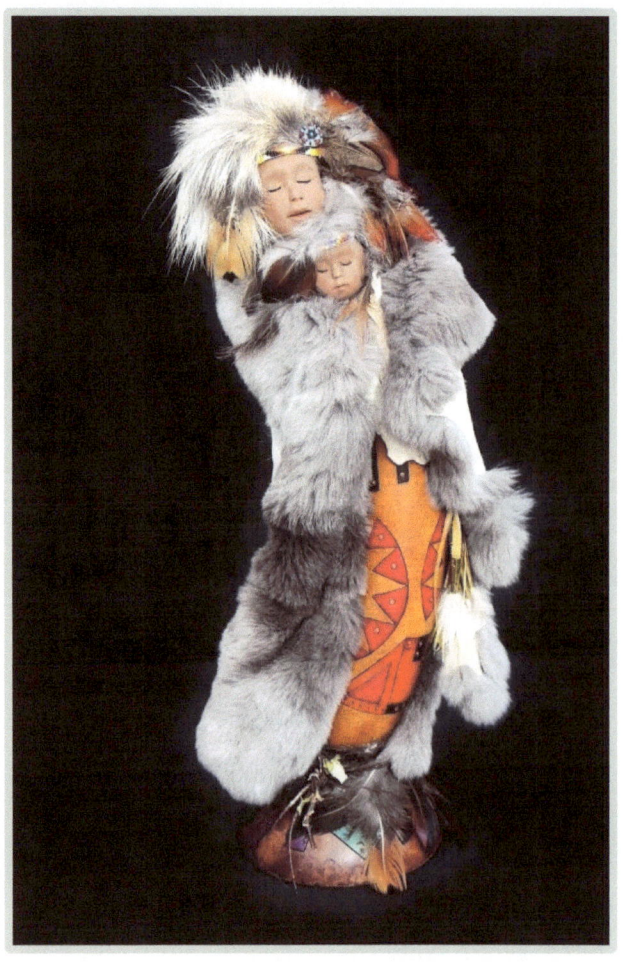

There is a segment of the population that for some reason thinks creating art dolls is a craft. The thought, the work, and the artistic skills that it takes to create these beautiful art dolls cannot be classified as crafts…….this is fine art! Check out the wonderful galleries where this 'fine art' is displayed and sold.

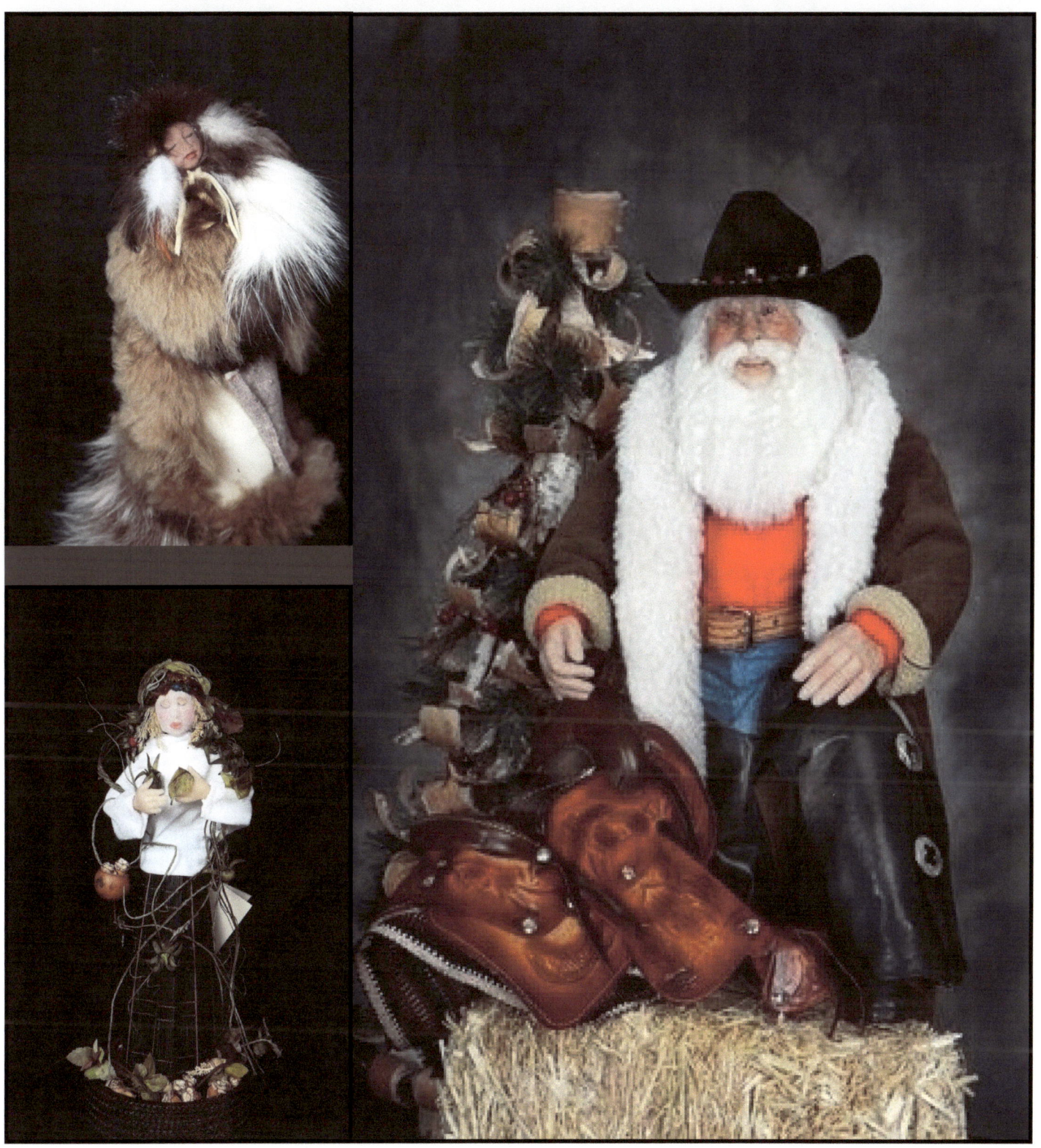

I Want to be a Mermaid
By: Margret-Ann Miller

Needle felted/no armature
20x15x12
www.therovingartist.com

I want to be a mermaid, but not for the reasons that first come to mind. No, I want to be a mermaid because their thoughts create the seas. Mermaids are creative, and their heads flood with so many ideas that there must be an escape, or the backup of thoughts will drown the poor things. During a full moon, they climb onto a sea stack and dangle their heads over the edge. As the moon crests, the moon rays kaleidoscope onto the mermaid's head and their skull cracks open. All their captive ideas turn into a waterfall and these ideas cascade into the body of water beneath them. This, my friend, is how all water that covers the earth came to be.

As mermaids are easily distracted, they must keep their eye on the prize. Concentration is vital as those pesky water squirrels will sit on the end of their tails, baiting them at every turn. On a moonlit walk on the beaches of Marblehead, Ohio, I spotted the ever-elusive freshwater mermaid on the rocks offshore! I crouched behind a massive boulder to watch the ceremony progressing before me. As she purged her ideas into the water, the lake foam lapped over my feet, and my mind's eye saw a myriad of art pieces just waiting to be born!

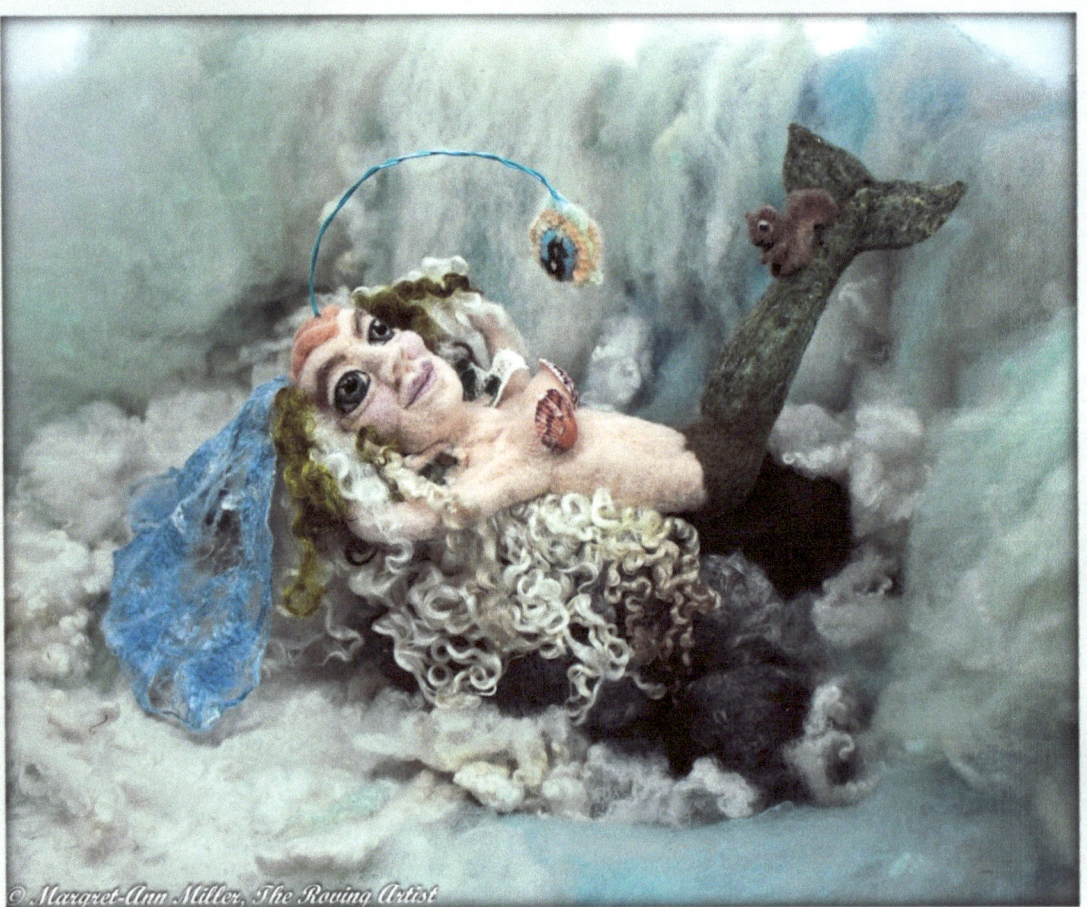

I quickly returned home to needle felt her likeness. Wensleydale locks were a perfect match for her milk-white hair. I hand-dyed roving to achieve her skin tone, and the wet felted mulberry silk matched the flow of ideas. Lincoln locks proved to be an uncanny match to the cliffs of Marblehead.

So, the next time you walk along the beach with the water swirling around your ankles, if you just so happen to have an AH-HA moment, close your eyes and thank the mermaids.

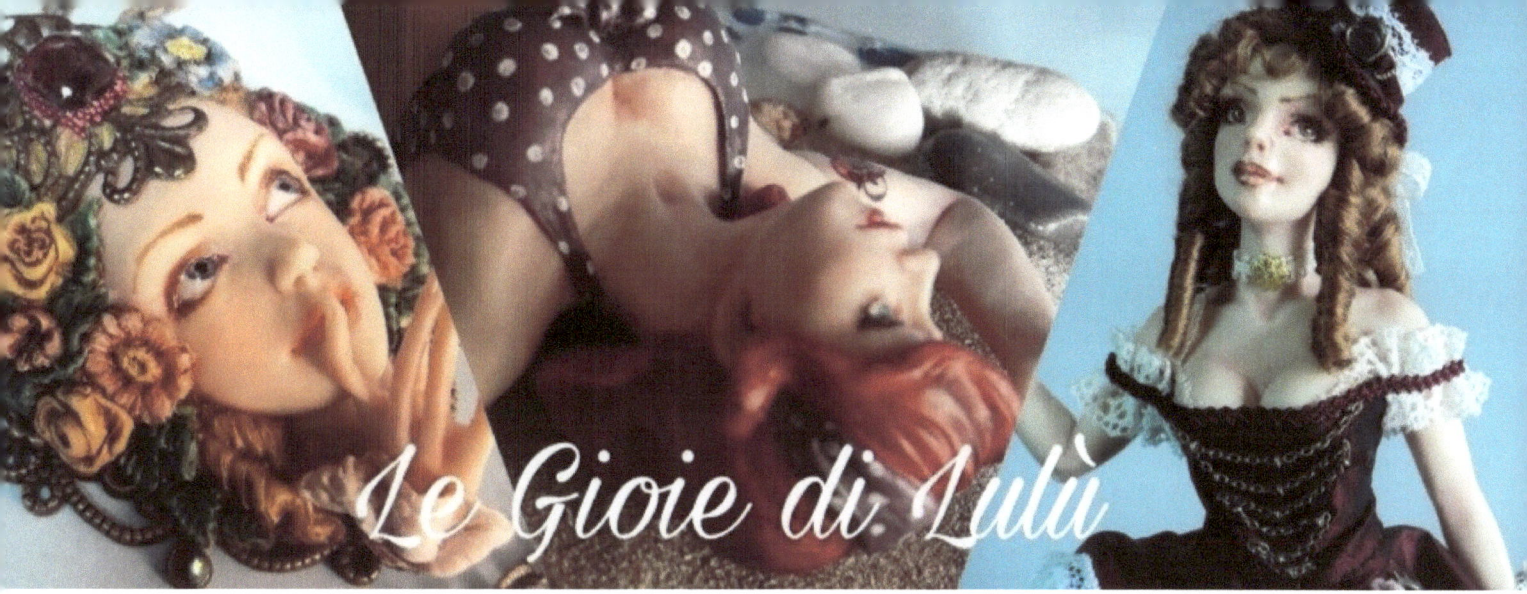

Loredana Salvo Loving Sculpting

I love art in all its forms, I studied sculpture, wood carving, painting, ceramic decoration and even tailoring and fashion modeling. I have worked in almost all these areas, especially the ceramic decoration that has occupied an important part of my life.

Three years ago I met the world of polymer clay that changed my world. I returned to my first true love "sculpture".

Now I create OOAK (one of a kind) on a 1: 6 scale. I like portraying women, but also fantasy figures such as fairies or mermaids, not even disregarding portraits.

I love this kind of creations because it allows me to exploit all the skills I have acquired over the years and at the same time to experiment with new materials and techniques. Every job is the result of a search to obtain more and more a result faithful to reality.

https://www.facebook.com/loredana.salvo.7

https://www.facebook.com/LeGioieDiLulu/

Tuffet Love by Gayle Wray

What you'll need:
- A doll-seat sized container
- Two coordinating upholstery fabrics
- Fancy upholstery trim
- A coordinating ½" trim
- Beacon's fabric tac
- Cardstock

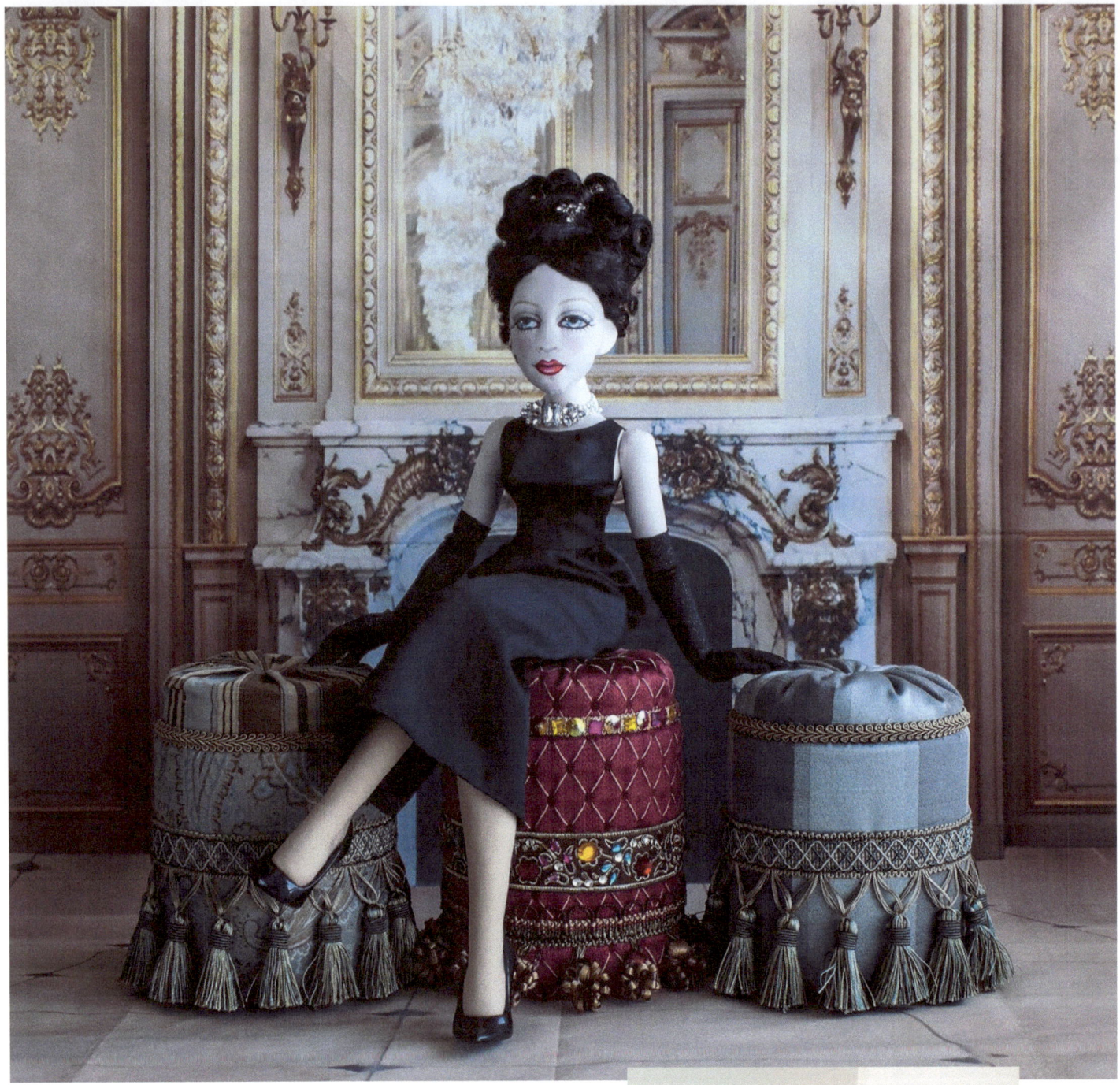

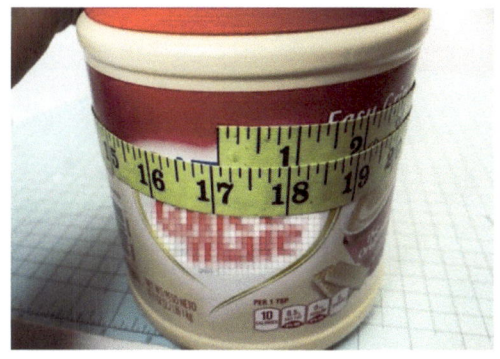 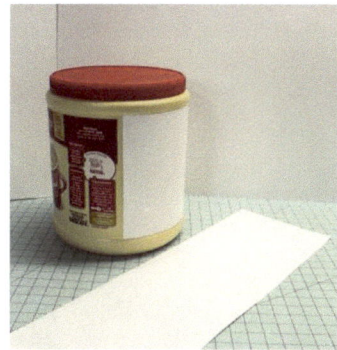 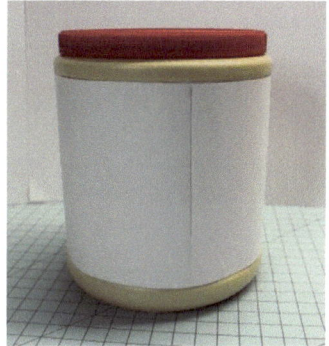

First, select a canister whose height is in scale with your seated doll. I found this nice coffee creamer container to use. Measure your canisters width, and cut apiece of card stock to mask labeling. Mine had 2 indents for gripping that I addressed by first coving them up, then I completely encircled the perimeter with the larger piece.

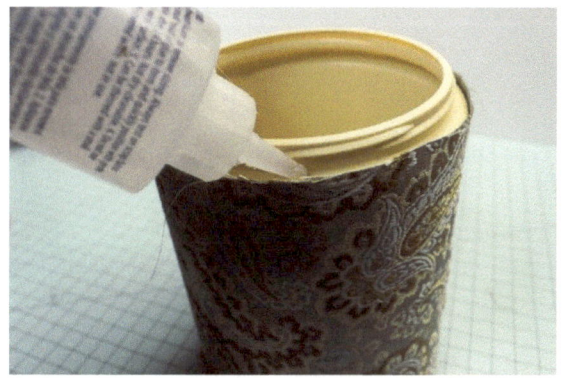 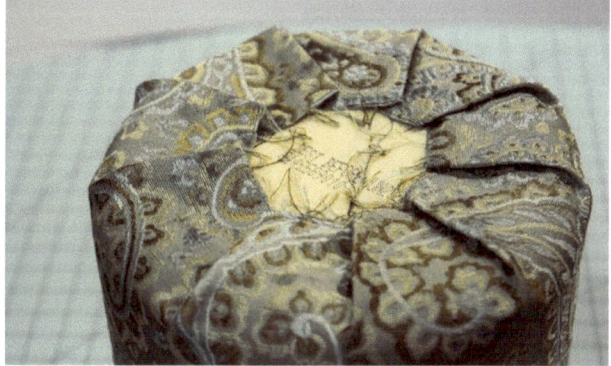

Then, cut a strip of your base fabric, long enough to meet the jars threads, and two inches longer than the bottom edge. Sew a narrow side seam, and glue to the rim. In a pinwheel fashion. And add a circle of felt or leather make a base.

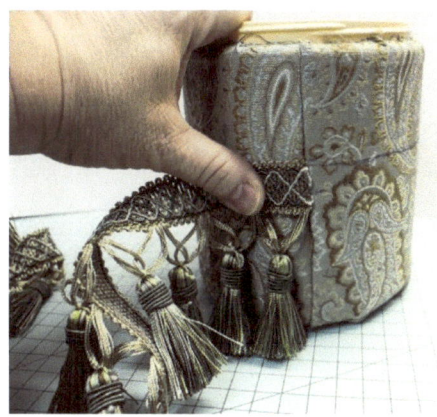 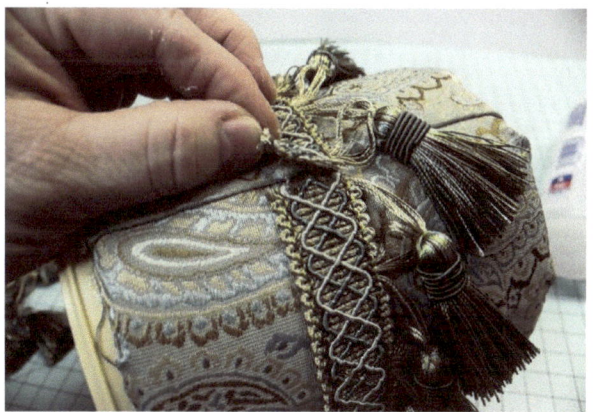

Mark a guide line with disappearing ink at a good level to show off a row of fancy upholstery trim. Glue the slightly overlapping end at the back seam.

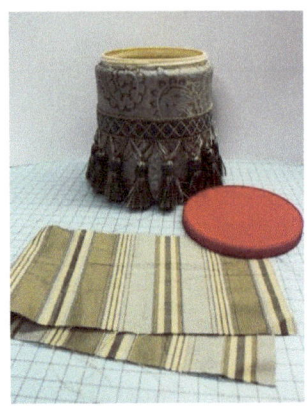 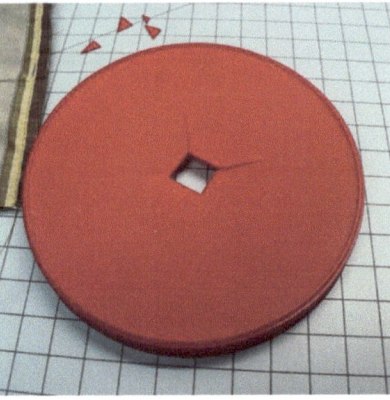 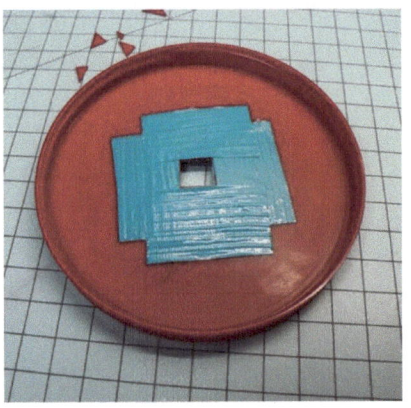

For the center gathered seat cushion, cut a strip of fabric that will be long enough to gather and pull through the center opening of the lid, I needed about 6". The lid was brittle, and cracked while piercing, so I reinforced both sides with strips of duct tape.

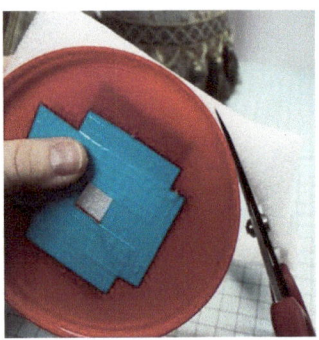 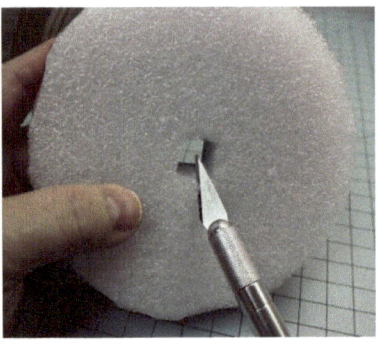 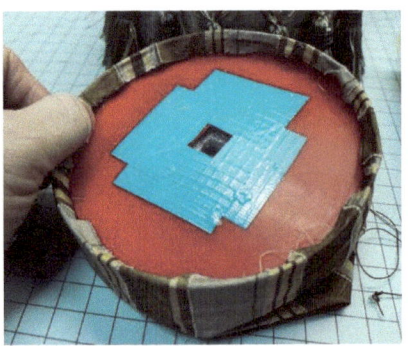

Use stuffing, or glue a 1" piece of foam to the top of the lid and trim around it, using the lid for a guide. With an Exacto knife, cut an opening to pull the gathered fabric through. Sew the cushion side seam, and glue it to the inner lip of the lid.

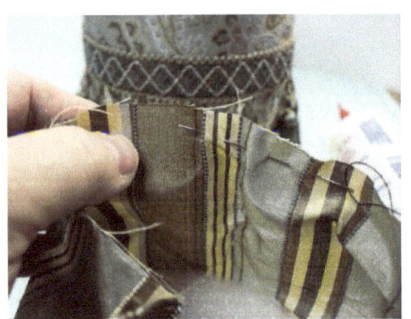 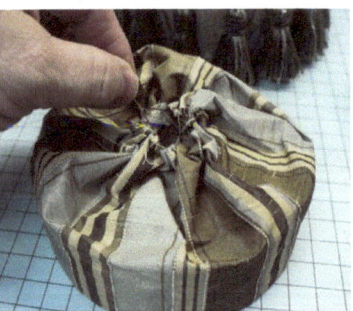 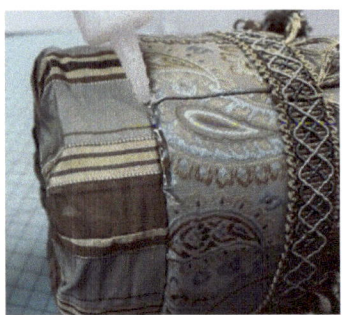

Loosely gather the top edge of the cushion fabric, and pull it to the inside. Add a fancy button to the center of the cushion and tie it off. Run a bead of glue around the inner fabric covered jar lid, and using the threads, screw the lid on. Finally, run a bead of glue around the side seam and cover the raw edges with a coordinating upholstery trim.
I've made these in many fun styles and colors. Each one unique and special!

For the first time, my "Making Angelina" doll making class (based on the printed manual) is **online**!

With over **50 videos** that will take you through each step of making your own Angelina. I cover all the sewing, stitching, and stuffing techniques, and also touch on needle sculpting, makeup, eyes and nails, and even cover wigs and clothing.

This is the same class I teach at my home and around the country. If you can't take the class with me in person, it's the next best thing to being there.

Angelina is a poseable, all-cloth art doll. She features 10 points of articulation: shoulders, elbows, wrists, hips and knees

Her measurements are:

- Height 21"
- Bust 8.5"
- Waist 6"
- Hips 10"
- Head 7"

She is an art doll, for adult collectors and not intended to be a child's toy.

If you already purchased the printed manual, you'll get a special discount for the new online class.

For more information go to:
www.gaylewraydolls.com

Highly Adored ....Accessories!!! ...
By Vikki Ebbeling

Accessories!!! Are like icing on a cake!!!
Without a doubt they absolutely change the mood of a simple black dress and add charm and interest to any art piece. We NEED accessories to perk things up! Without them is like a day without sunshine. If you want your art to pop out and speak accessories are a good way to do it.

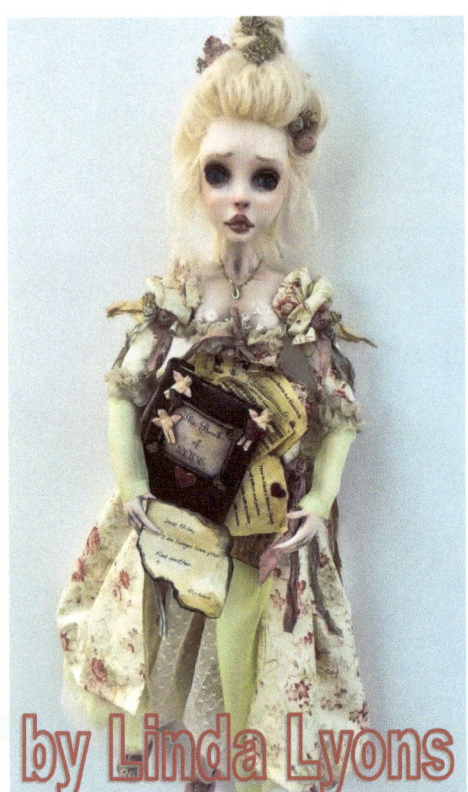
by Linda Lyons

How to accessorize and where to buy them:
There are so many second hand boutique shops that have amazing clothing with old buttons, silk ribbons, feathers and fabrics that we cannot even buy in regular stores any more.
The textures and colors of lovely brocades, silks, and satin fabrics from boutique clothing can also be made into hats, belts, and bags and many other thing without costing a whole lot.
Little earrings, bracelets and necklaces can be made from old broken jewelry. There is always something you can salvage from them. Antique shops are wonderful! They have unique pieces of accessories that have survived over many years and many articles having acquired natural patinas that can add super charm to an art piece. There are many craft stores that recreate antique and vintage trinkets and the newer "bling" pieces for extra sparkle.

We can create many things with polymer clays such as beads, broaches and shoes. Embellish them with our findings from flea markets to little second hand shops. Be creative and let your mind go wild with ideas.
Do not be afraid to try new things. Allow yourself time to experiment. Some things might not work out so well but you might find yourself delighted with what you've created with your own hands. Just have fun with it. Relax and do not stress yourself. You will come up with some amazing ideas. Keep in mind what you want your art piece to say. It must speak from your heart.

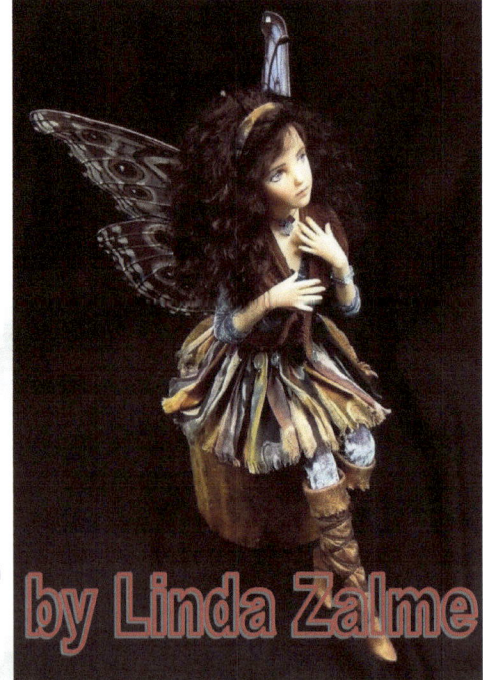
by Linda Zalme

Nothing will speak louder than a beautifully accessorized art! Yes, we all seem to like the little extra fling from old to new. All accessories have the potential to add some elegance and charm to a beautifully sculpted piece or any other medium used to create art dolls or art figures/figurines. They add interest and a special statements to our final creations. Sometimes old accessories with a little touch of new added to them will make wonderful eye catchers ...bringing interest from our viewers. older folks and the younger generations as well.

Just adding a little piece of furniture ,decorated boxes or books. little glasses or perhaps a small cane will do it or a fancy head piece could also add lots of charm.

A small accent piece might be all we would need.
No matter how small or how big they are.... they are a must!

Elizabetta Visentini

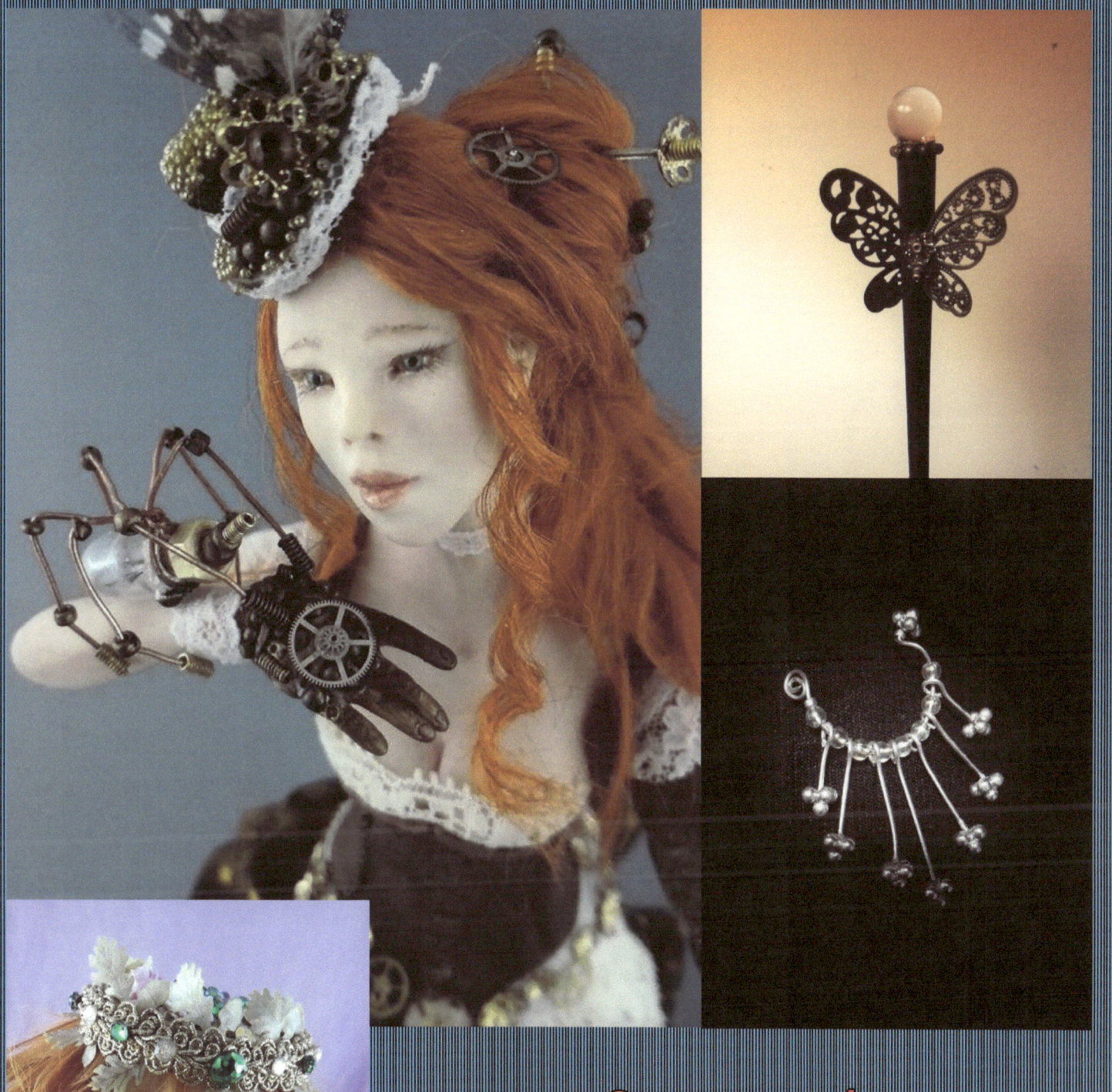

Steampunk

and

Fairy Accessories

Fabric Mushroom by Lisa Wroblewski

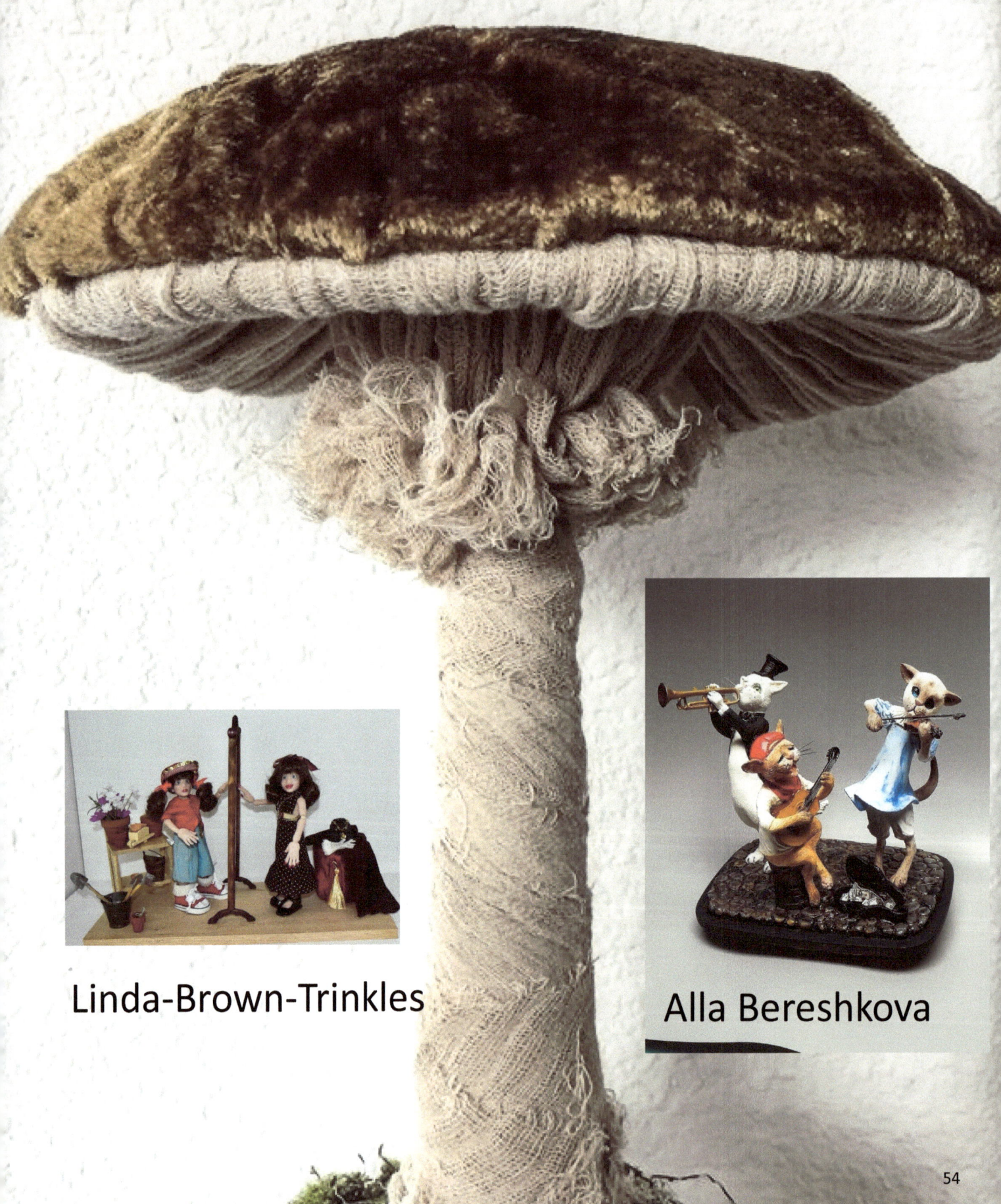

Linda-Brown-Trinkles

Alla Bereshkova

Patrizia Cuzzo

Shares accessory ideas

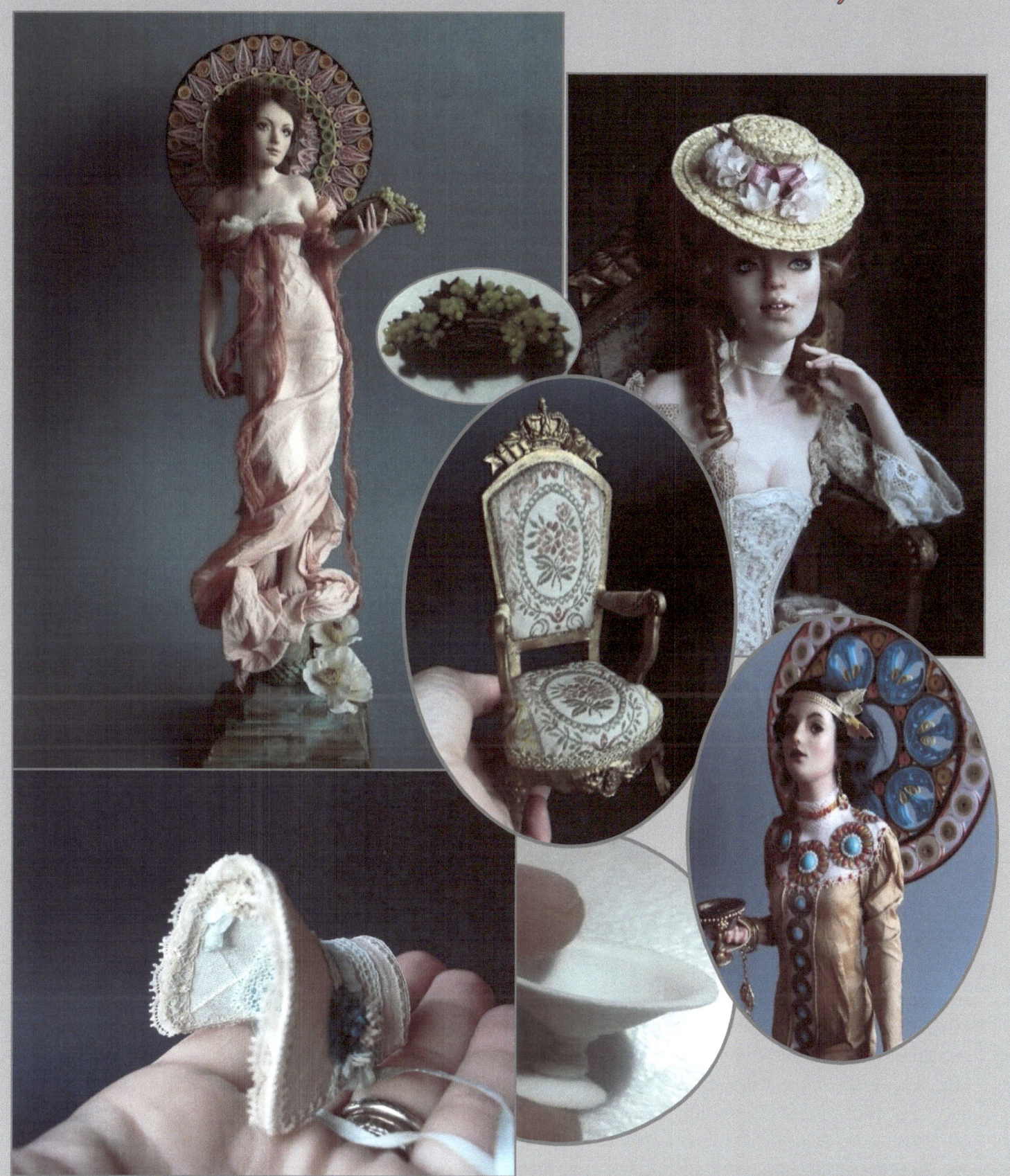

Ankie Daanen
A Master at Costuming and Accessories

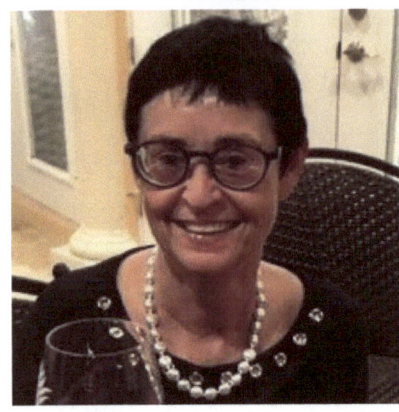

Inspiration from Ankie

A Pinnacle Award Receiver from the Professional Doll Makers Art Guild

I cannot imagine my life without dolls and dollmaking! I am never short on inspiration and I have more ideas in my head than I can make in my life! Looking through `doll-eyes´ at the world is how I see every day. I believe that the basics of dollmaking is excellent craftmanship but also it actually goes beyond this. Dollmaking involves expression and recognizing emotions together with using high quality materials, so this means dollmaking is a never ending story.

From my studio in Spain, where we live, I work on my creations daily, trying to make the ultimate doll that communicates everything I want to say. Being a workaholic, spending 9 hours a day making dolls, preparing classes, working on on-line classes and doll-related things, I experience never a dull moment!

One of the most important elements is to infuse my creations with a soul. Dolls with a soul are my passion. I like my dolls to be happy, sad, humoristic or even mystic. They should give you a feeling that they have a life and soul, and that they bring to you an intimate connection as if they have a human spirit. Recognizing this soul contributes to the experience of looking at each doll as a piece of art.

My passion for dollmaking and artistic pursuits began very early in my life. I was born in The Netherlands and even as a child I was always looking for beautiful things. I think I wanted my life like being in a fairy-tale. Growing up with only brothers I did not share my fantasy world, but my dolls became my best friends! As a child I was constantly searching for ways to express my artistic abilities. My mother sewed my clothes and a large part of my childhood was spent seated beside my moms sewing machine, waiting for left-over scraps of fabrics to make ballroom dresses for my Barbie dolls. This great love of fabrics still remains today. I get inspired by beautiful materials, laces and trims to design my costumes. Initially my dream was to have a career as a ballet dancer, opera singer or designer. Unfortunately my parents at those days did not share this idea of going to art school. So I attended an educational academy and became a teacher. After teaching for five years I began searching for an opportunity to express my creative energy. I was attracted to the conservatory where I studied music and I became a music teacher. I undertook this career for 13 years, but was still searching for something more, not knowing what that should be.

Then I visited a doll exposition!!! I went there to take a look and was blown away! Seeing these dolls hit me right in the middle of my heart. This was what I wanted to do! After returning to that exhibition three times I realized that my passion in life was to become a dollmaker! That doll show changed my life! In my pursuit of the craft I began to take dollmaking lessons and soon I started to teach myself. Nowadays I like to work with Creative Paper clay and porcelain. I love the charm of a very smooth skin, which I can achieve with both. Through the years of being a dollmaker I developed my own style and many, many students experienced this in my classes that I teach all over the world. Also once or twice a year I teach dollmaking holiday classes in Spain as well as private classes in my studio and also once a year I teach together with my colleague Marlaine Verhelst a special five day class ´The Dutch Touch" in the USA. My dolls have brought me all over the world and I have met so many lovely doll friends. My goal is always to create the ultimate doll. The doll that will stay in your memory after you have seen it!

ankiedaanen@hotmail.com

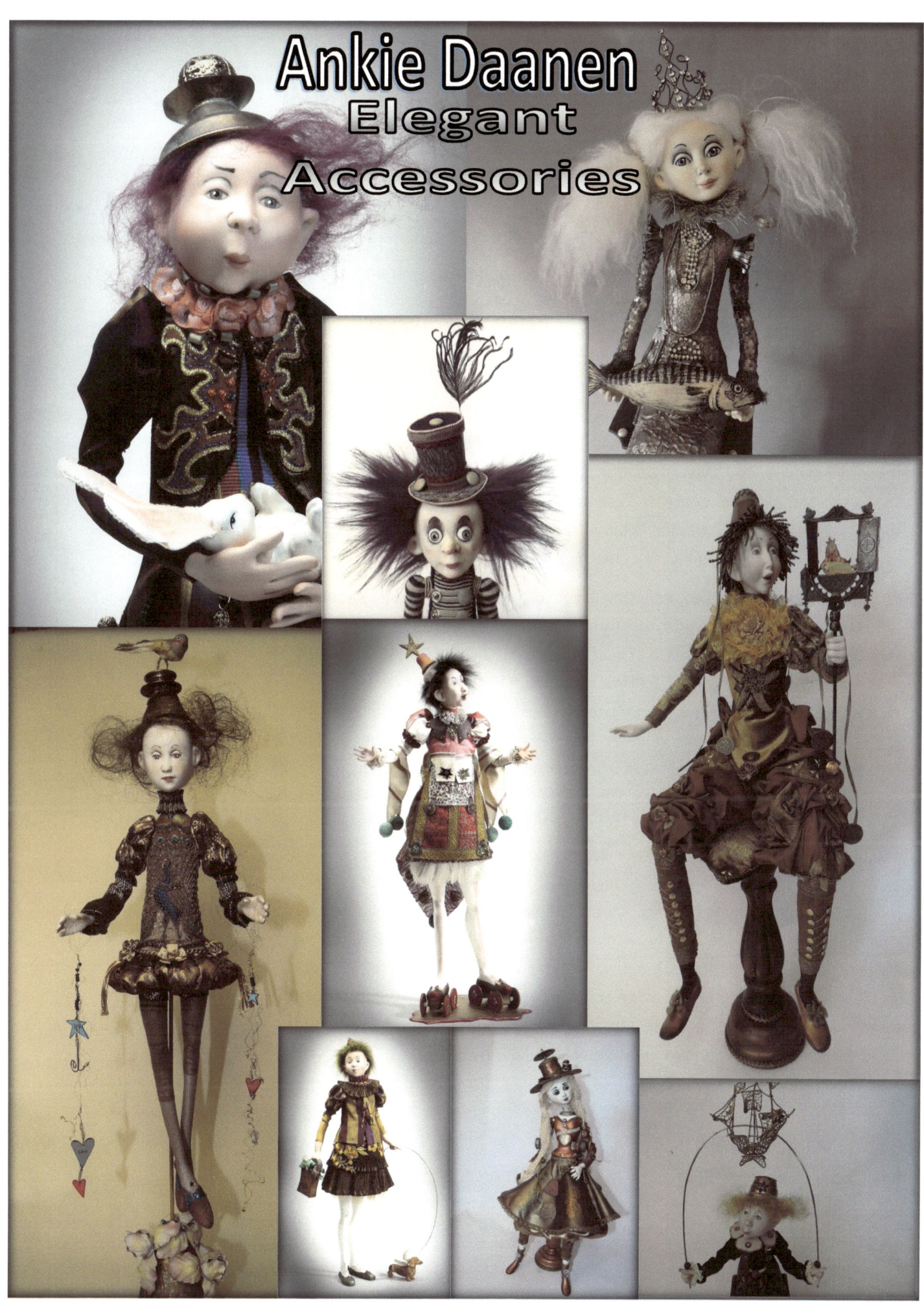

How to make high heel shoes

By Ankie Daanen

Take the two pieces of wire for the shoes/legs and bend them double. Than you bend them into the right shape. Take masking tape and the skewer and take the bended pieces of wire and attach with small pieces of masking tape the skewer to the wire. Cut the cardboard soles and attach these to the front of the foot. Take care that you have a left and a right foot!! Now we take the paper clay and add some clay in the middle of the foot. Now put some clay on top of the foot. Do NOT take too much clay. You can better add some clay if it´s not enough than having too much to start with. Cover the little pieces of the skewer. Then cover the under leg with clay. Make two little balls chicken-pea-size, and these will be the heels. Make the upper legs and calves bigger/wider. What I advise is to let the legs dry. I always like to sand in between the sculpting stage s, because you can see very well if everything is symmetrical.

You can speed dry the clay. I use a simple convection oven for this. My advice is to put it on the lowest heat, which mostly is 100 to 150 degrees. Open the lid and put the parts you want to dry ON TOP of the oven or ON THE OPENED LID. NOT INTO the oven. Especially not parts from styrofoam like the head or the body, because the styrofoam will melt immediately! Now we again attach some clay on top of the foot to give it more volume. Next we cover with a thin layer of clay the bottom of the shoes (the soles). Let it dry and sand it again. You can use a strong sanding sponge to flatten the soles. This will be a big help to make the doll stand well. Add some clay over the heels and make them both the same. Maybe the top of the foot can have some extra clay too. Now take the styrofoam body and both legs and see if they are long enough. Maybe if you want legs a bit longer. you just add some clay to the legs. Make the calves a bit bigger. Make two very thin rolls of clay long enough to go around the instep of the shoes. Push on the table one side of the roll in the length a bit flat, take it from the table, wet it and put it around the sculpted foot and blend it in. You need a sharp pointy tool to poke holes into the body to be able to attach the legs. There are many different ideas for shoes It all depends on how you put the roll over the foot. Have Fun!!

Shoe Design

In Paper Clay

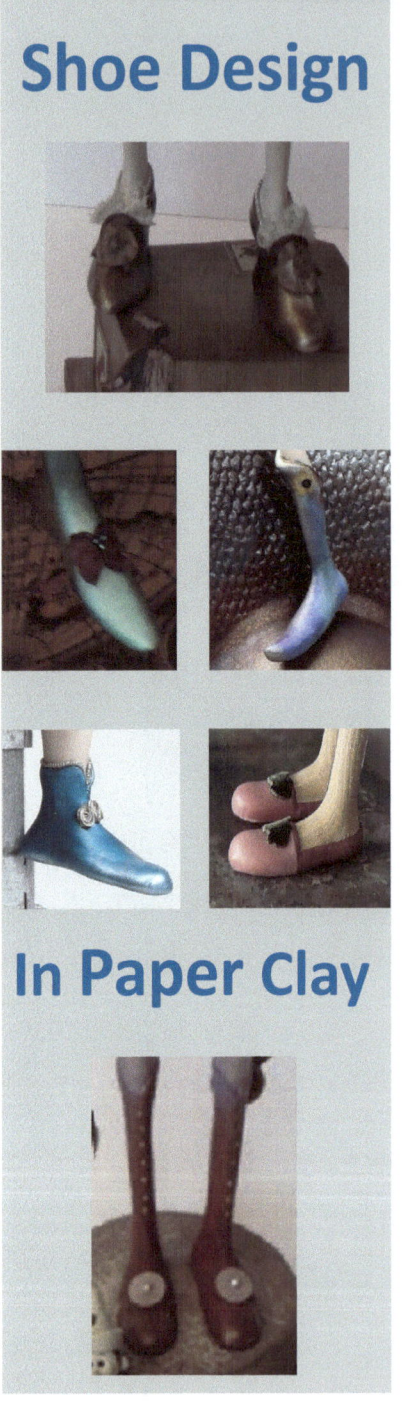

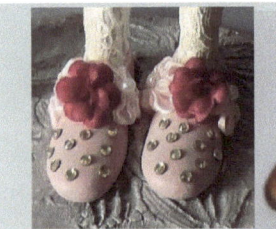 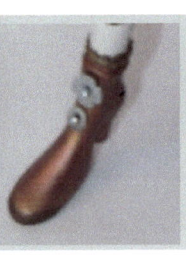 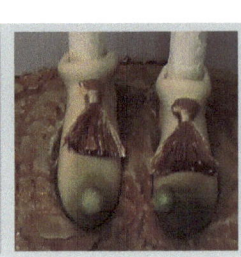 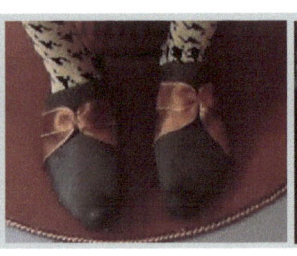 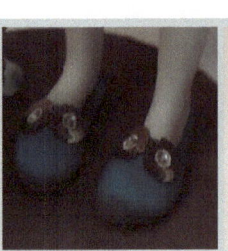 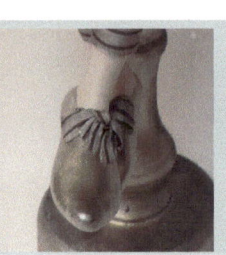

"Cherie"
by
Phyllis Morrow

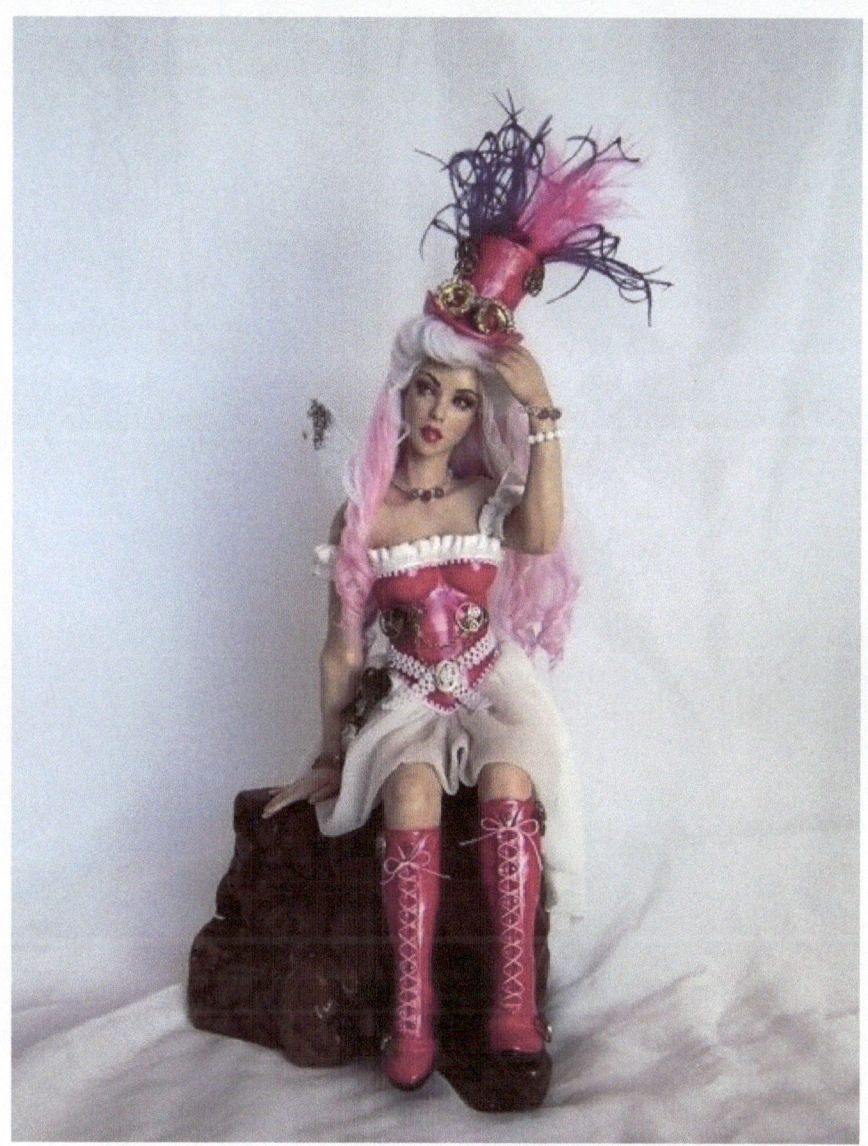

Cherie is a One of a Kind Steampunk Sculpture that is sculpted from polymer clay. After I sculpted and painted her I was ready to make and apply all of her costume.

Her eyes are a beautiful purple with a dark pink rim, so this set the theme of colors. I also love pink so much that I decided to do most of her in a bright Magenta color but with a touch of purple. Her hair was applied in locks with strips of pink and purple throughout the white. I thought this would blend in the pink and purple theme. Her boots were sculpted out of clay and painted the Magenta pink. I added little gears from watches to give them the steampunk look. I applied micro beads to the front of the boots to use as lace hooks for the laces to go around and lace up the front. I love this look. Her vest was sculpted from clay and painted the same Magenta pink to look like leather and match her boots. I then added watch gears and chains to the front of the vest for decoration. I applied two keys to her belt so she has them handy. One key to start her steampunk car and the other to open the door to her little house. Her skirt is a simple one that is short in front and longer in the back to keep up with the new styles. I made her skirt from silk gauze. Most of my cloths or costumes for my sculptures are made with silk gauze. It lays to scale and can be easily dyed any color. The white ruffles at the top of her vest and on her shoulders is also sculpted from clay. I have added tiny micro beads to top off the look. All her jewelry is made from chains and beads that she has collected. She always keeps an eye open for these little treasures. Her hat is sculpted from clay and painted to match her vest and boots. I made her goggles from two eyelets. I took the two eyelets added clay to make the nose bridge and then a thin strip of leather for the side ties. I then added clear liquid gloss to the inside of the eyelets to form the glass. Pearls were attached around each eyelet to make them more glitzy. She wears these when she is flying around so putting them on her hat keeps them close at hand. More gears were added to the hat and a big plum of pink and purple feathers top off the look. Her wings were made with fantasy film to give the translucent look with steampunk gears to add to their decor. She sits quietly on a rock waiting for her good friend to pick her up for a day out together.

phyllis@pgmsculpting.com

World Famous Bill Nelson

Shares His Ideas

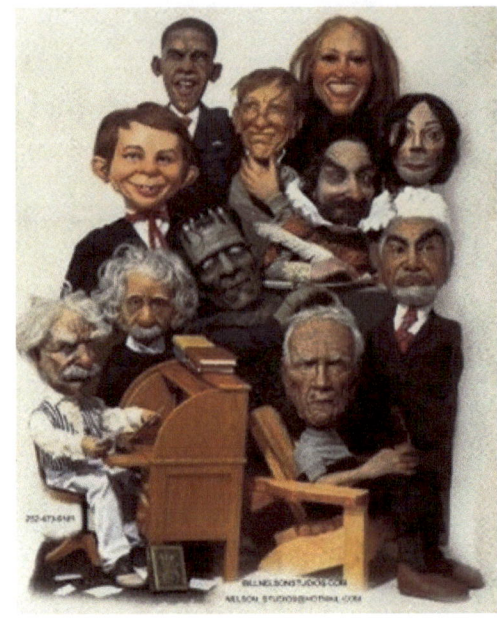

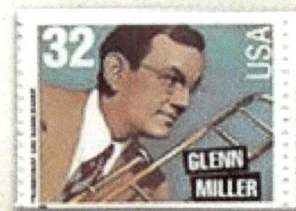 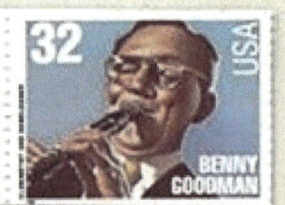

Bill Nelson's illustrations have won over 900 awards including two gold medals from the New York Art Director's Club, and two silver medals from the Society of Illustrators, which used one of the winning pieces for the cover of their 28th Annual. His work has been profiled in Step-by-Step Graphics, and American Artist.

In addition to a fruitful illustration career, Bill is an internationally recognized sculptor and ventriloquist figure maker. His one-of-a-kind figures and automata have made their way into the private collections of Demi Moore, Whoopie Goldberg, David Copperfield, Bruce Willis, and Richard Simmons, among others.

Bill Nelson is listed in Who's Who in America. He currently lives and works in North Carolina.

Classes Available

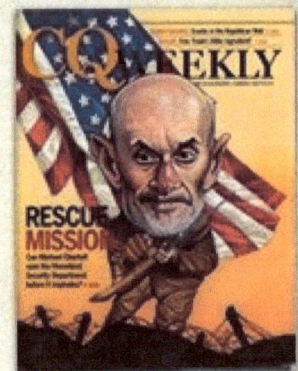

Bill Nelson is an internationally known illustrator and sculptor. His award-winning illustrations have graced the covers and interiors of The New Yorker, The New York Times Book Review, Newsweek (10 Covers), Time, TV Guide and The Atlantic Monthly, to name only a few. His advertising clients include Estee Lauder, Columbia Pictures, Sony Records, Gore-Tex, Reebok, Bolla Wine, The Kennedy Center, David Copperfield, and Demi Moore.

He has exhibited in numerous galleries and museums worldwide, including the Norman Rockwell Museum, where he exhibited a series of Big Band illustrations created for the United States Postal Service.

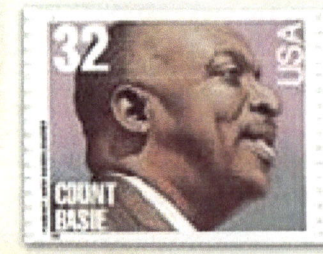 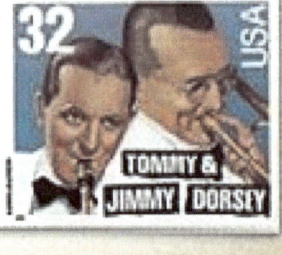

Bill Nelson is a receiver of the Pinnacle Award from the Professional Doll Makers Art Guild

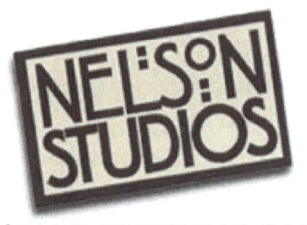

BILLNELSONSTUDIOS.COM

Many faces of Bill Nelson

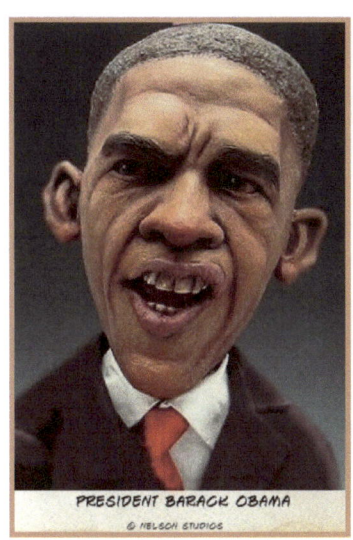
PRESIDENT BARACK OBAMA

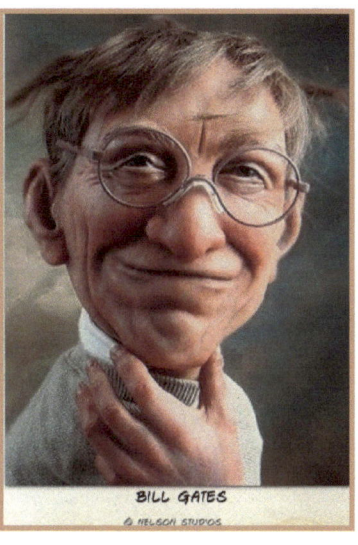
BILL GATES

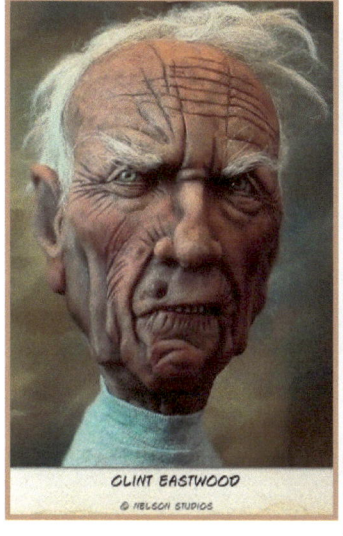
CLINT EASTWOOD

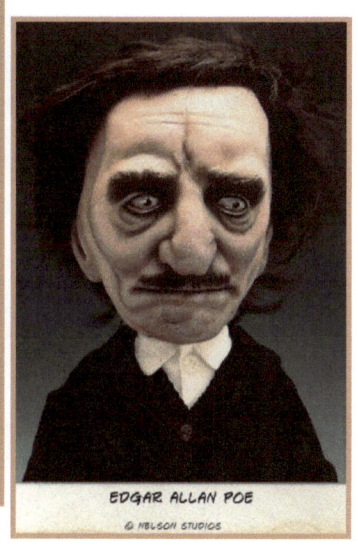
EDGAR ALLAN POE

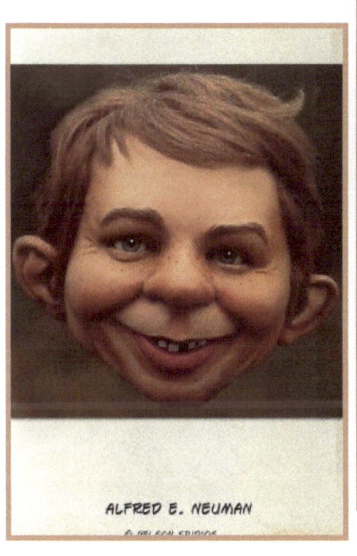
ALFRED E. NEUMAN

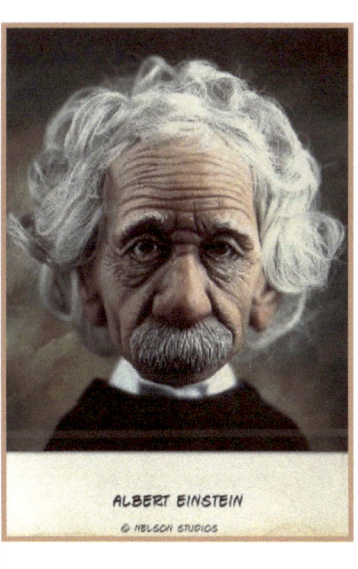
ALBERT EINSTEIN

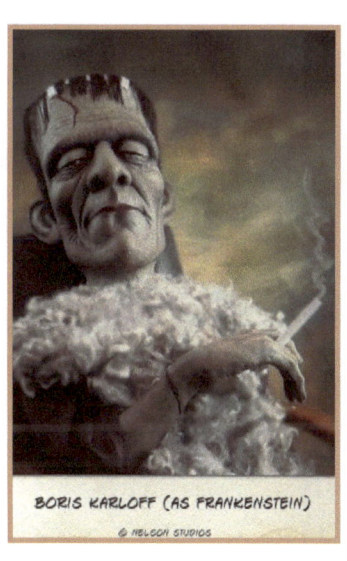
BORIS KARLOFF (AS FRANKENSTEIN)

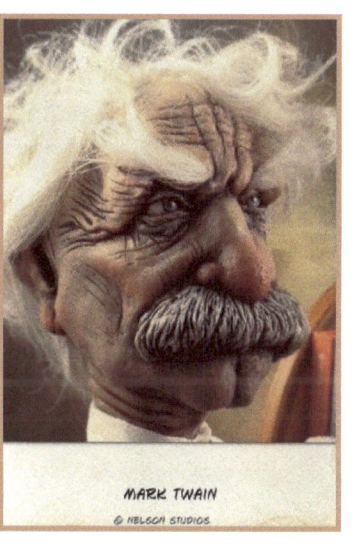
MARK TWAIN

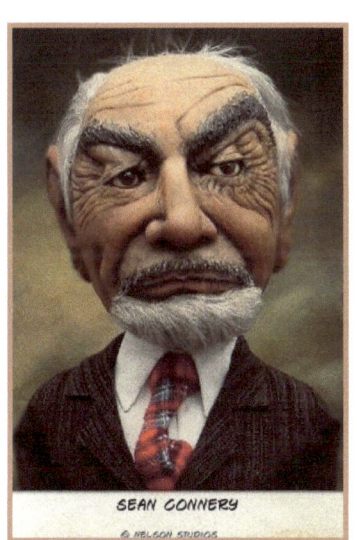
SEAN CONNERY

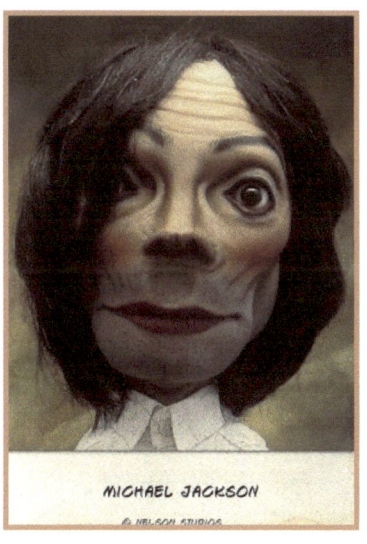
MICHAEL JACKSON

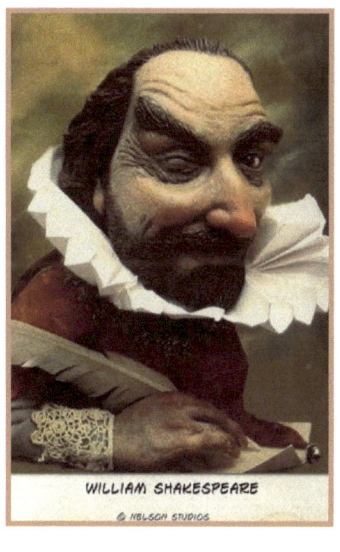
WILLIAM SHAKESPEARE

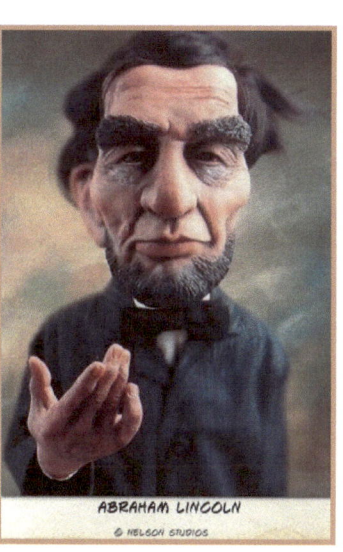
ABRAHAM LINCOLN

Libra Opal Mermaid

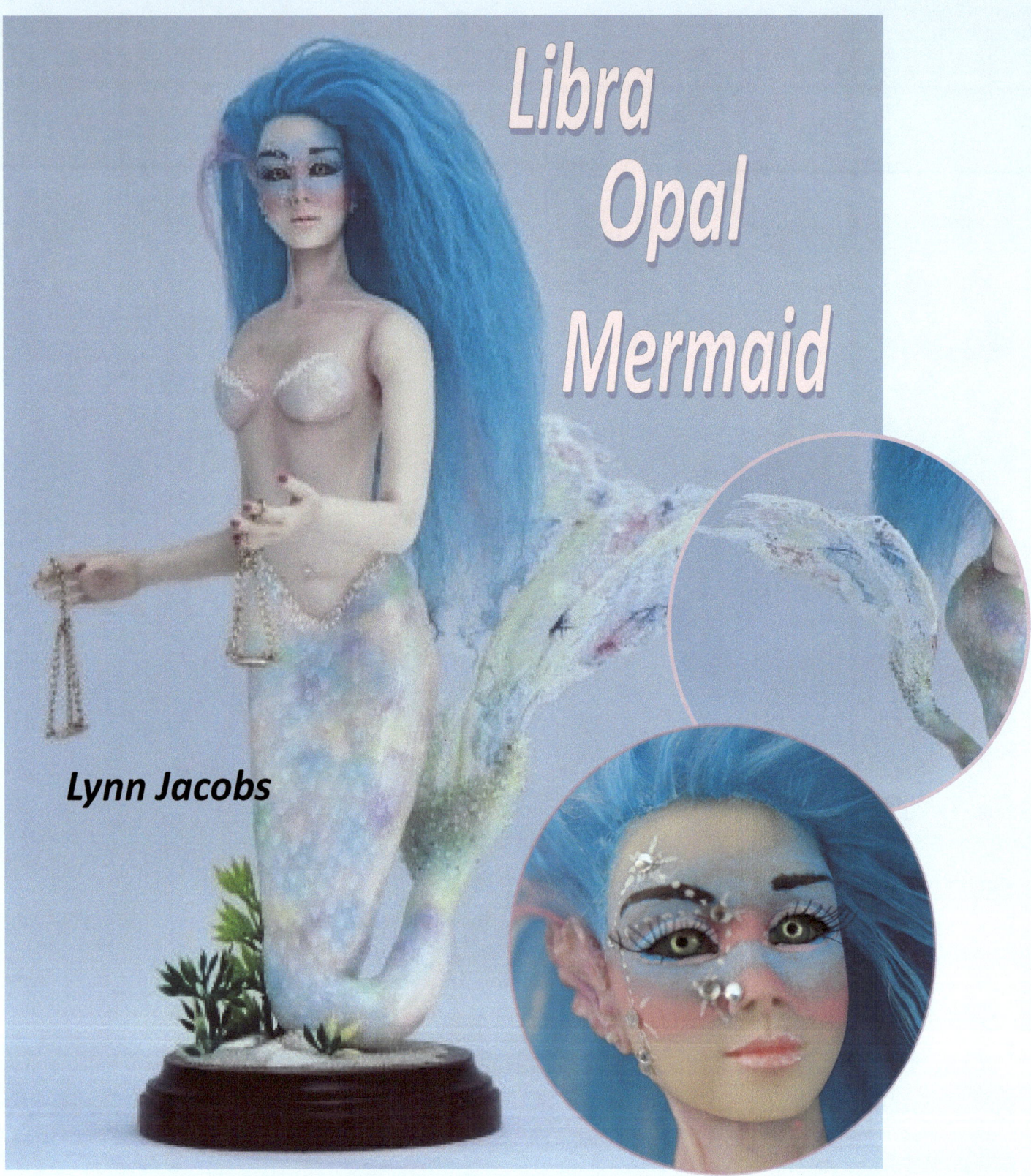

Lynn Jacobs

I finished my first polymer clay art doll, a mermaid, in September of 2015. This is my newest doll, Opal (I am a Libra) and she is my 9th art doll, completed on July 31, 2018. She is 10" tall including the base. She would be 17" from the top of her head to the tip of her tail if she were standing. I created the eyes myself. Her tail-fin is made of lace. Her eyelashes were applied individually and she's wearing pearl earrings. Genesis paints were used for her coloring and makeup. A crimping curling iron was used to create the texture in her hair. (Please see how her tail was made in separate article.)

artbylynnjacobs@gmail.com

Making an Opal Mermaid Tail

By Lynn Jacobs

Opal was inspired by my zodiac sign, Libra. Libra's colors are light blue and light pink. For her Opal tail I started with Fimo Effects Translucent White and added just a tiny bit of Fimo Professional in different colors making separate clay pastel shades. I also created a clear pile with just a tiny bit of white mixed in (Photo 1).

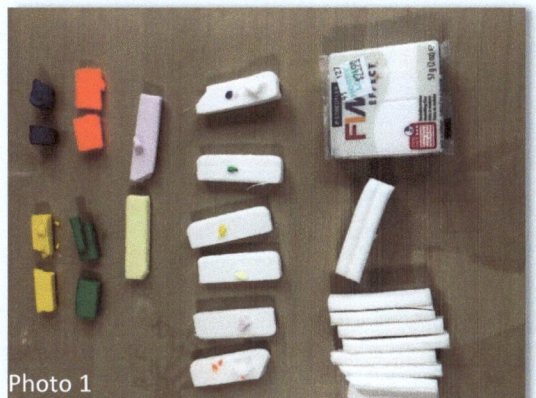

Photo 1

The first batch was too dark so I had to add more translucent. The flat pieces on the right (Photo 2) are too dark. (I'd added more colored clay). The round balls on the left are after I added more translucent and a very tiny bit of white Fimo Professional, for a more pastel effect. The Fimo Effects Translucent White is known to produce moonies and it's suggested that adding a bit of white helps reduce them. Then I made a pile of tiny bits of each color and pressed together for a sample and baked (Photo 3).

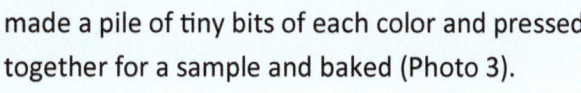
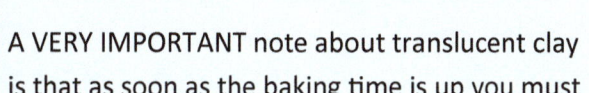
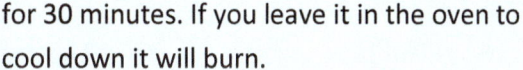

Photo 2

A VERY IMPORTANT note about translucent clay is that as soon as the baking time is up you must immediately take it out of the oven. You can (gently) put it in an ice water bath for 30 minutes. If you leave it in the oven to cool down it will burn.

After the success on the sample, I moved onto the doll. I again chopped up each color into tiny little bits and then gently tossed them all together in a big pile. After applying liquid Polyclay all over the tail, I gently picked up clusters of these mixed colors and loosely placed them all over the tail area (Photo 4). When most of the tail was covered with the loose bits of clay... starting at the top at her waist and working down, I pressed the clay onto the tail, making sure air pockets had a way to escape. When I got to the fin area, I inserted the fin and added a thin layer of liquid Polyclay to thin and pressed/mixed/blended the clay into the lace where it joined and slightly over the edge of the lace. For the scales effect, I was inspired by a tutorial by Phyllis Morrow of PGM Sculpting. After smoothing the colored bits of clay, I then applied a thin layer of translucent clay to the entire tail, smoothed, then created the scales. I added a bikini top, created scales there also, and baked.

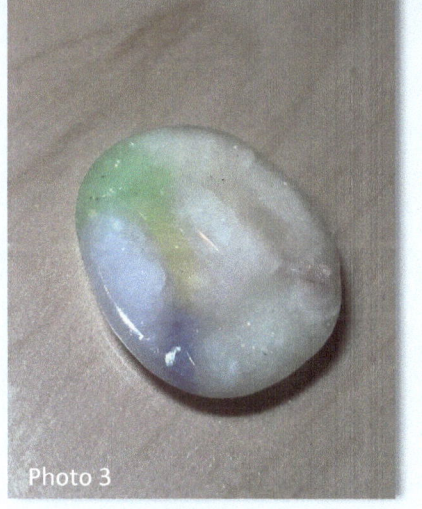

Photo 3

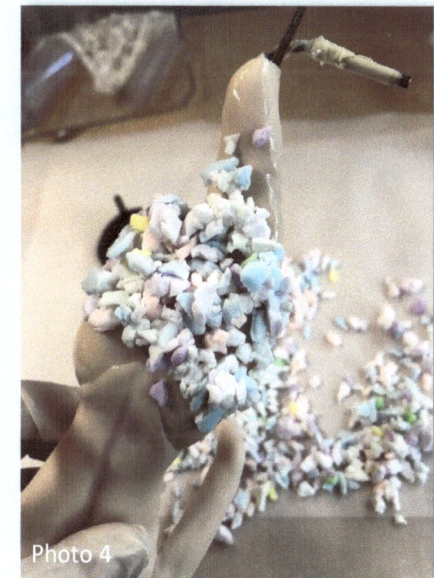

Photo 4

Directing the Viewer

How to use color, pattern and accessories in Dollmaking

By
Lynn Jacobs

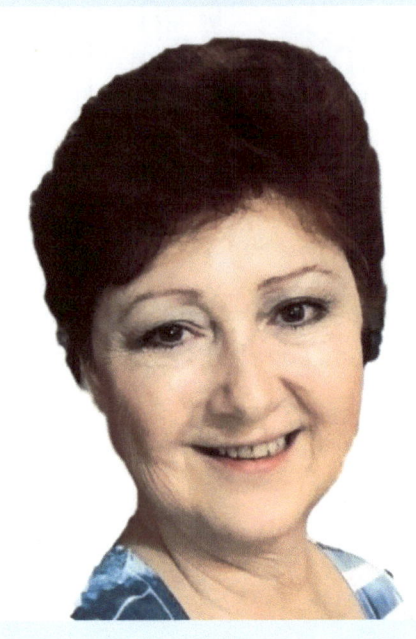

I was a master hair colorist for 27 years (now retired) and am thrilled to realize I can continue my love of color and pattern with my new doll-making artistic adventure. Color harmony can make certain colors/textures pop and make others appear to recede. For instance, do you want the clothing to be center of attention, or the face? You can use color choices to bring attention to the cleavage or the legs by where you place your stronger and softer tones.

You can direct the eye to one area as a dominant focal point, or you can arrange your colors, patterns and accessories in order to have someone's eyes move from one place to another, and even rest at one area or detail for a moment and then move on. You can actually control what you want admirers of your work or potential buyers to notice.

Brightly colored or white ruffles along the top and/or shoulders when all the rest of the dress is subdued will call attention to the upper half of the body. A flower or shiny object placed right at the point of interest attracts the eyes to that particular area. Earrings bring attention to the face/ears/eyes, but place sparkly red shoes as the dominant color on her and the attention is drawn to the feet. When you want your own eyes to stand out you are more meticulous about your eye makeup, but when you want the attention to be drawn to your lips you would soften the eye makeup and brighten the lipstick.

Color choices can help enhance the final effect you're after. Color can help elicit mood of your piece. Softer, delicate, pastel tones/colors/patterns softens and makes a piece appear more feminine, delicate or innocent, whereas bold vibrant colors are more demanding/powerful and can take attention away from minor flaws.

This reminds me of the class I went to about a woman with a glass eye... everyone noticed her glass eye until the colorist placed a big bold color right above that eye. People's eyes were then drawn to the hair color instead of the glass eye.

Soft/pastel tones on a big strong manly man only serves to soften it's masculinity, it's power. Rich, earthy tones and/or vibrant intense hues creates an impression of strength or boldness. Color can be used to help in choosing eye and hair color, makeup, clothing and accessories so they all work together in harmony.

A very valuable tool is a color wheel. They have instructions on how to use them and they make coordinating colors a lot easier. Opposites on the color wheel make each other pop... such as red and green (think Christmas). Yellow is soft next to orange or red, but pops when placed next to blue and yet pops even more when yellow is placed next to violet/purple. This is because of it's relationship to each other on the color wheel.

When I'm thinking of my next sculpt I'm already wondering which eye color will enhance the overall effect I'm after. Do I want it to enhance the clothing/color scheme by having (for instance) light blue eyes with light blue clothing, or do I want light blue eyes to pop but have her face appear softer (for instance) by having dark blue or yellow, muted orange or red shades in her clothing? Remember that darks appear to recede, whereas lights come forward, and brights dominate. You can even create a creepy, uneasy feeling in your piece, thereby making your creepy doll even more compelling by your color (and pattern) choices… think about how creepy a doll you could make using color disharmony, such as a pastel Spring-like dress on a zombie child. The colors clash, the expression on the doll, the materials used, all maximize the creepiness factor.

Something which helps me easily figure out which colors work well together is to think of the colors during certain seasons. Winter includes clear deep cool tones, such as ashy browns to dark brown to black, true-white, true red, clear blue, cool green. Spring colors include clear light warm tones such as pastels like lavender, pale yellow, pinks, light blues. Summer is soft, light and cool such aqua, turquoise, cool blues and greens, soft grays. Autumn includes the deep warm tones of oranges, olive greens, gold instead of yellow, cream instead of true white, and rich warm browns. You can add bits from the opposite season depending on the effect you're after.

You can help move the eye in different areas of your sculpt by how you choose and place color and texture. In Louise Crone's dress, for instance in photo 1. The white stands out first and grabs attention (even though it's a WIP not ruffles at the moment), but the details of locks, stars and chains draw the eye all around the piece, resting on the added details… you have to know even in this early stage that this will be a fantastic piece. Even the vertically striped bottom draws the eye down, but it immediately draws the eye back up to the other details. IMO this is masterful use of color and texture.

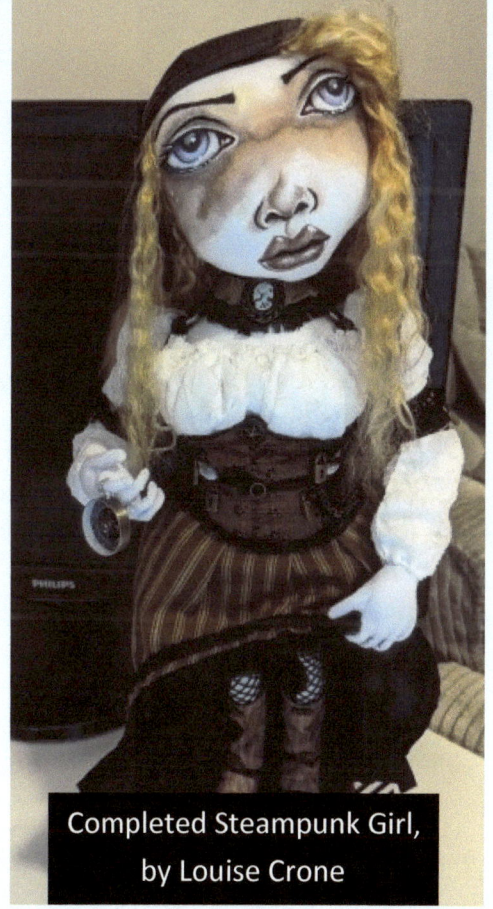

Completed Steampunk Girl, by Louise Crone

WIP—Steampunk Girl, by Louise Crone

I asked Louise how she came up with such a wonderful combination of colors and accessories and she explained, "I start with my head full of ideas, write down what I can, and start from there." Louise has a supply on hand which she goes through first, before going shopping for other pieces. She said, "I love detail and colors so love to shop and work it all out putting fabrics together to work out what will go and what colors/patterns for what character I'm working on. When I put pieces together they could be different colors/patterns but I try to match what works." And she explained that she may try several different pieces until she gets just the right combination.

65

photos. Realize that dark colors recede while light colors come forward, and bright colors "pop". Color can be used to convey mood and attitude… Sunshine yellow, baby blue, red hot red, pretty pink, bright white, cream.

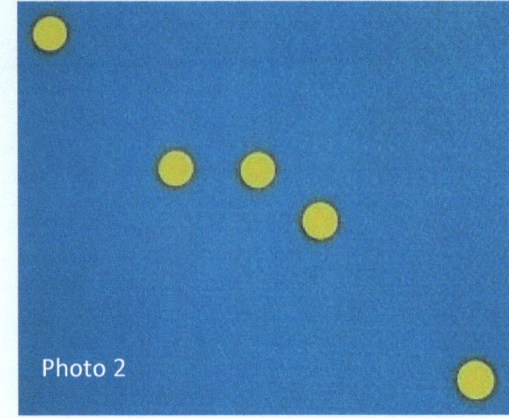

Photo 2

Notice how your eye moves diagonally across the entire page in photo 2, yet it pauses on the center 3 dots because they're close together. So, when you want the eye to move swiftly across or past something keep the area uneventful and/or directed past it, but when you want someone to appreciate a detail or remain in an area a little longer you can place a "busy" pattern such as multiple small items arranged near each other or use a horizontal pattern to break up or pause at a spot on a vertical. Verticals draw the eye up and down, horizontals draw the eye side to side and diagonals draw the eye across.

In this image (photo 2) I was going for a relaxing, gentle effect on the eyes. The background is neutral blue with it's triadic yellow (on the color wheel). Notice how your eye calmly travels from the top left to the bottom right, with a minimal pause on the 3 center dots.

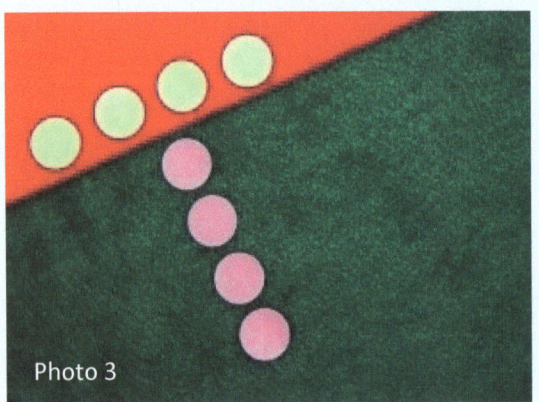

Photo 3

The bright red in the this third photo commands your attention, your eyes pause on the diagonal pale green dots, yet you're drawn to the pink dots and then back up, momentarily resting on the green dots again because of the side to side motion, and quickly back down and up again. The dots could be buttons, circles, diamonds or diamond-shapes, triangles, etc. They could be stitched patterns in pieces of cloth, pieces of leather, bare skin in an outfit, pretty much anything. You could change the color scheme for a less dramatic effect and yet still control where the viewers eye travels. Imagine the effect if the green dots were bright yellow or orange or black, or reversed. The point is that with color and pattern you can guide the viewers eye towards areas you want to show off, such as workmanship or parts of the anatomy, or you can draw the eye away from an imperfection by minimizing the area.

In this fourth example notice how your eye reacts to those assorted patterns. Try turning it sideways and upside down to see how your eye continues on a path. Do you follow the path but pause to bounce back and forth on the same ones again and again? Mixing colors and patterns adds more interest and keeps the eye busy hopping from one to another. You can also create a sweet innocent doll by using primarily pale, neutral colors/patterns. Now imagine how you could place your pattern for a dress using shapes to direct attention. You could use circles, squiggles, the sewn pattern in the cloth, contrasting colors or monochromatic color combinations.

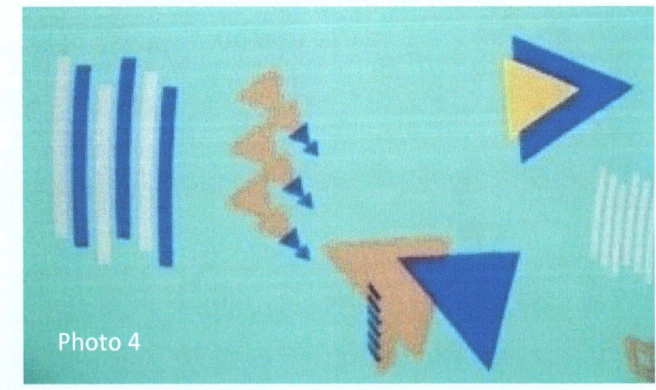

Photo 4

I hope you've enjoyed this intro to using color, pattern and accessories, and that you'll have even more fun creating purposeful harmony and movement in your doll creations.

artbylynnjacobs@gmail.com

ACCESSORIES ARE ONLY AS LIMITED AS YOUR IMAGINATION

WOOL ART DOLLS

by Cherie' Davidson

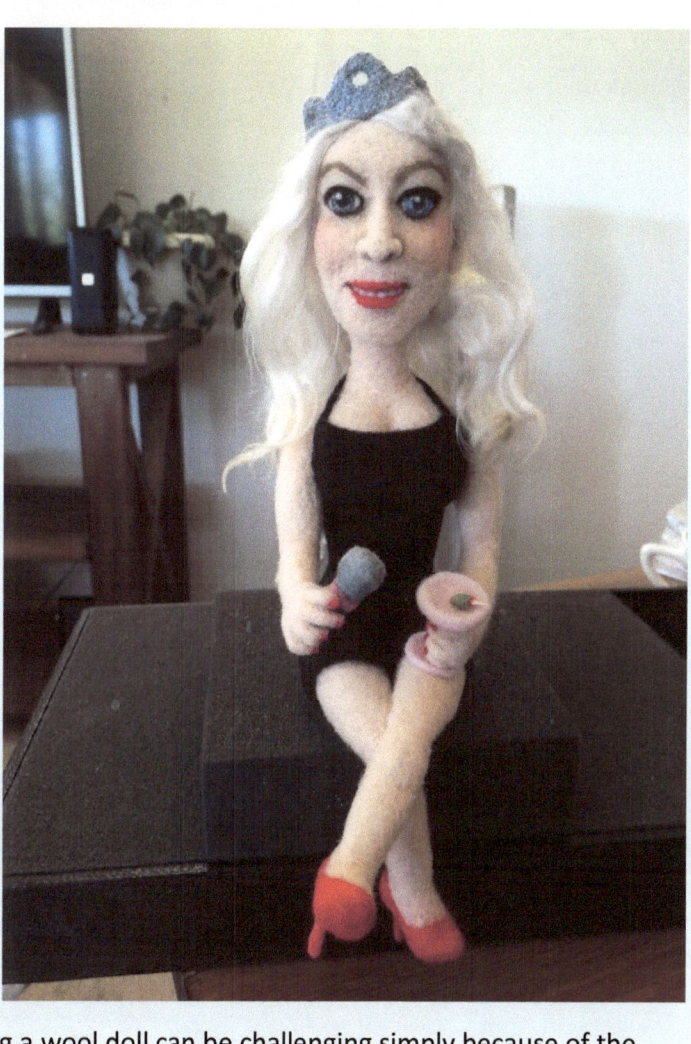

Accessories for dolls are not unlike decorations on a cake—they add unique character, provide story, texture, life... and take the cake from what any bakery can sell to a one-of-a-kind creation that makes an indelible impression on those who see it. This is what your unique accessories do for your dolls. It gives them an immediate story, and makes an emotional connection with those who see them. Accessories can make all the difference to a buyer, taking them from admiring your skill, to feeling they have to own your incredible creation, and show it off!

Whether subtle, or elaborate, accessories should not be overlooked. They are part of your signature, part of that doll's special message, its magic. However, with that stated, all accessories are not necessarily the standard things like handbags, hats, elaborate bling. Really meaningful accessories can be as subtle as outstanding detail, or a prop that makes the entire piece sing.

This is true for any medium chosen; and the more creative the medium, the more challenge...and the more magic that results. For sculptural needle felt artists, sculpting a wool doll can be challenging simply because of the material. Wool as a sculpting medium can be fussy, and requires great patience. It takes many, many hours and thousands of stabs to needle felt a full art doll. But, the doll is not where it should end. It may take time, but please don't forget the accessories, for that is where your doll transforms into something truly special, and elicits murmurs of wonder from those who see it.

Mixing media and techniques can be an eye-popping way to accessorize. For instance, a needle felted doll might have a bit of tapestry needle felted as part of a coat, or a fancy footstool for her to rest her foot on. My medium is 100% wool and needle felting. It's unusual for me to use other materials, but I love to incorporate natural wood or other natural fibers. One of my early dolls was for a songwriting friend who loves to think of herself as a hard-working, hard-playing part-time princess. So I sculpted her alter ego from wool, all wool. Of course she needed a tiara, but what else? I needed just a little something else, so it added to the inside joke, but didn't take away from the doll. She enjoyed partying, so I decided to needle felt her a martini...little green olive and all. But even though I love the challenge of working all in wool, that martini had a real wood toothpick skewering the wool olive. That toothpick, which was so small and seemingly insignificant, was noticed by almost everyone! And that was the little accessory that made everyone do their "oohs and ahhs" and mention that doll.   Detail....accessories are about detail, about charm, endearment, sentiment, surprise—the unexpected magic. Think about what special touch, magical signature, you can add to your doll. What perfect accessories will tell the world your doll's one-of-a-kind story?

cherie@darlingirlcreations.com

THE ANGEL DOLL COMPANY

- **Learn to Sculpt**
- **Reborn Babies**
- **Doll Kits**
- **Paint A Friend**
- **Collectibles**
- **Silicone Doll Art**
- **OOAK Dolls**
- **Special Events**
- **Birthday Parties**

45 N. Market St.
Lancaster, Pa 17603
717-947-4328
theangeldollcompany@gmail.com

www.ingramcontent.com/pod-product-compliance
Lightning Source LLC
Chambersburg PA
CBHW051203220526
45473CB00003B/882